BRITISH GUN ENGRAVING

BRITISH GUN ENGRAVING

TEXT BY DOUGLAS TATE
PHOTOGRAPHS BY DAVID GRANT

SAFARI PRESS INC.

Tate, Douglas

Second edition

Safari Press Inc.

2000, Long Beach, California

ISBN 1-57157-166-3

Library of Congress Catalog Card Number: 99-71024

10 9 8 7 6 5 4 3 2

Printed in China

Readers wishing to receive the Safari Press catalog, featuring many fine books on big-game hunting, wingshooting, and sporting firearms, should write to Safari Press Inc., P.O. Box 3095, Long Beach, CA 90803, USA. Tel: (714) 894-9080 or visit our Web site at www.safaripress.com.

TABLE OF CONTENTS

DEDICATION
&
ACKNOWLEDGMENTS

To Bonny Hawley-Tate . . .
the love of my life

Hundreds of people have helped with this project. Prime among them are the connoisseur collectors who allowed their guns to be photographed. They asked to remain anonymous, but I would like to thank them, for without them this book would not have been possible.

To all the British engravers who took the time to send photos and personal histories I send heartfelt thanks. They, too, made this book work.

There were a number of others who made important contributions, and these include the staff of Christie's Arms & Armour department, past and present: Chris Brunker, Peter Hawkins, and Howard Dixon, who helped greatly with the essay "The Early Years"; David Trevallion of Shooting Sportsman; *the Ladywood Shooting School in Wiltshire, England, for making available so many of the hammer guns that appear in this book; and Peter Scott Edeson, Shaun Cole, and the staff of the Victoria & Albert Museum, South Kensington, London.*

Jan Roosenburg of Holland & Holland in New York provided many of the photos for the essay on the relationship between gun engraving and the Arts and Crafts movement. Raj and Jeet Singh helped with the images of Indian guns. A very special thank-you goes to Geoffrey Caspard and Ken Hunt, Harry Kell's apprentices, who were a vital source of information and images for the essay on their former master.

It is likely that I have forgotten some names. To those people, I apologize for the oversight.

INTRODUCTION

There are devotees of first editions, vintage motorcycles, Cuban cigars; my passion has been British game guns. A love of shooting, a lifelong enthusiasm for the history and aesthetics of double-barreled shotguns, plus an indentured apprenticeship as a photo engraver made it inevitable that I would one day write this book. But why now?

The generosity of the anonymous collectors in allowing their guns to be photographed made this book possible, so to answer the question "Why now?" may, perhaps, be best expressed by one of the collectors. This collector, a genuine connoisseur of engraving but not necessarily an Anglophile, told me why he had booked so many engraving slots with the Brown brothers and Phil Coggan. "We came to realize that, just as Kornbranth, Fugger, and the Austrians had dominated engraving in the thirties, Louis Vranken and the Belgians had done so in the fifties and sixties and then the Italians, under the influence of Fracassi, had led the way in the seventies and early eighties, Britain now leads the world."

The other half of that "we" is a friend and rival collector who showed me examples of Italian engraving he had commissioned a decade ago. The images, although mirroring nature precisely, could be viewed only from a specific angle because the cuts were so shallow. "To get the look we see in glossy magazines" he told me, "they fill the engraving with ink while it's still in the white. The result is fantastic when viewed from one angle, but it does not last." He showed me recently engraved guns in which background detail was so finely rendered that it began to disappear. "The best of the Brits make deeper cuts while retaining realism. The result is textured, permanent, the finest in the world." Few who see this book would disagree.

Martin Smith's game-scene engraving on the floor plate of a Westley Richards double rifle.

PART ONE

English engraving before the Mantons was either crude or foreign, or, as in the case of this Turnpike blunderbuss by G. Taylor of London, both. Some very high-quality gun embellishing appeared in England before this time, but aesthetically it has its origins in continental Europe.

Chapter 1

THE EARLY YEARS

The defining difference between the traditional London best gun engraving and its Continental counterpart is that the former is viewed as conservative and the latter as opulent. There is no question that this is a reflection of national character, but the image also ignores an essential, and often overlooked, distinction: In Europe, gun engravers grew out of the silver- and gold-smithing crafts, while London's engravers came from the printing trades.

While flamboyant and even ostentatious gun decoration was the norm, say, in France, with its court artisans proficient in the decorative arts, the need in book publishing for clarity, lucidity, and most important of all legibility led English engravers to a simpler style. If Boutet's guns are the heirs of Cellini's salt cellar, Manton's are the descendants of William Caslon's bookplates.

Although the link between graphic arts and gun engraving can be seen at virtually any time in history, it was strongest

The Royal Cipher on a military firearm like the one engraved by William Caslon for three cents. Note the number of cuts.

at the end of the eighteenth and the beginning of the nineteenth centuries. It was then that the distinctive, and indeed conservative, nature of British gun engraving was being established. Certainly there had been lavishly engraved English guns prior to that time, but they tended to copy Continental forms.

The most famous Englishman who ever engraved guns was undoubtedly William Caslon (1693–1766), whose fame came from his genius for designing typefaces rather than for engraving guns. Nevertheless, Caslon had begun his working life as a gun engraver for the ordnance department at the Tower of London. He was born in Halesowen (today an extension of the Birmingham conurbation but then a town in Shropshire) in the West Midlands, a town then as now with

A perforated brass sideplate on a blunderbuss by G. Taylor, crudely engraved.

gunmaking connections. During the nineteenth century Halesowen supplied Birmingham with its gun barrels. Today it is a source of gun cases.

At the age of thirteen Caslon went to London, where he was apprenticed to Edward Cooke, a freeman of the Worshipful Company of Loriners. Loriners (or lorimers) were the craftsmen who made metal horse bridles, spurs, and stirrups, and as early as 1538 a traveler to Birmingham described it as a town of "many lorimers that make bittes." The Loriners had a strong contingent of gunlock engravers, and Edward Cooke was then the main contractor to the Board of Ordnance at the Tower of London. He was paid four pence (approximately three U.S. cents) for every musket lock engraved with the royal cipher.

When Caslon completed his apprenticeship, he was given a similar contract, though at a reduced rate: "A contract with William Caslon for Engraving repaired Musquet locks (according to the plain pattern) 500 at 3 pence each." He was also paid four pounds and twelve shillings for repairing the Gunmakers Company proof marks and for making a copper printing plate with their coat of arms on it.

In Johnson Ball's comprehensive biography, *William Caslon (1693-1766)*, he writes that "Caslon was engaged on gunlock-graving on his own account for three years at the most, 8,400 locks in round figures passing through his hands in this period, bringing in approximately £105, or £35 a year." This was not the decoration of ornate sporting guns—at least none has come to light—but rather the tedious and repetitious striking of "His Majesty's Cypher & Crown with the Broad Arrow & date of Year." Each piece was identical to the next and required many hundreds of cuts with the graver.

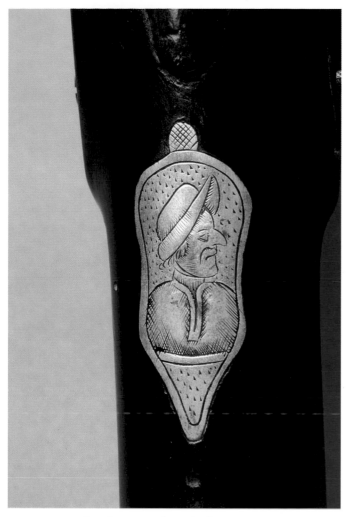

A caricature head engraved on the brass escutcheon plate of the Godfrey Taylor blundebuss. These were in fashion from 1675 to 1690.

Caslon next became involved in the manufacture of book-binders' punches, which cut letters and ornaments in relief on brass punches for hot leather pressing, a task in which a stamping die eliminates what was previously a monotonous task. The inescapable conclusion is that Caslon's experience led him to a world in which dies and punches consigned repetitive hand engraving to obsolescence. Today, of course, military firearms are still marked with the modern-day equivalent of a cipher, but Caslon would be pleased to know that the work is now done with a stamp.

Caslon's genius eventually emerged as a designer of type faces, another task in which a tedious business—in this case writing—is simplified by impress. We musn't forget that in medieval times if one required five copies of, let's say the Bible, they were laboriously copied out by hand. Printing eliminated the tedium of writing, and Caslon's work improved printing. His typefaces were easy to read and masterfully simple. One was chosen to print the American Declaration of Independence in 1776, and "Caslon" type is familiar today to anyone who reads the *New Yorker*.

An almost exact contemporary of Caslon's was John Pine (1690-1756), who may have been a pupil of the great French engraver Bernard Picart. He is best known for his series of plates representing the defeat of the Spanish Armada from drawings by Clement Lempriere, chief draughtsman in the Ordnance Office at the Tower of London. But his real significance, as far as gun engraving is concerned, was that he was the master to which the Mantons' gun engraver, William Palmer, was initially indentured.

William Palmer (1737-1812) was born in St. James, Piccadilly, London, to the wife of a breeches maker and was apprenticed to Pine in 1753. Three years later Pine died, and Palmer served out his indentures with John Searle,

Palmer's houndlike dogs appear dozens of times in his book of rubbings. All have similar stylistic elements in common with this dog on the buttplate of a single-barreled fowler by John Manton.

A hare in its form on a single-barreled John Manton. Based on Albrecht Durer's famous etching, the hare is identical to one in William Palmer's book of rubbings and is one of the images that make identification of the engraver certain.

a stationer whose business he may have eventually taken over. Certainly by 1762 Palmer was established as a writing engraver, and his move to larger premises and his willingness to take on numerous apprentices—seven in all—suggests a successful business. We can get some idea of the variety of work Palmer's shop may have turned out by this account by Thomas Bewick (1753-1828) describing his apprenticeship with Ralph Beilby:

> I was kept closely employed upon a variety of jobs; for such was the industry of my master that he refused nothing, coarse or fine. He undertook everything, which he did in the best way he could. He fitted up and tempered his own tools, and adapted them to every purpose, and taught me to do the same. This readiness brought him in an overflow of work, and the workplace was filled with the coarsest kind of steel stamps, pipe moulds, bottle moulds, brass clock-faces, door plates, coffin plates, bookbinders' letters and stamps, steel, silver, and gold seals, mourning rings, etc. He undertook the engraving of arms, crests and ciphers, on silver, and every kind of job from the silver smiths; [he] also engraved bills of exchange, bank notes, invoices, account heads, and cards.

In addition, Palmer engraved gunlocks. We know this because of the discovery of one of Palmer's account books by Evan Perry in 1972. These accounts, which cover the period from 1791 to 1794, record engravings executed for Henry Nock, Durs Egg, Robert Wogdon, John and Joseph Manton, and several other established London gunmakers. The real significance of the book, however, at least as far as

The pineapple filial on the John Manton single-flint fowler is typical of guns of the era.

Opposite page: A single-barreled flintlock sporting gun, circa 1806, by John Manton of Dover Street, London, a 17-bore with 33-inch barrels. This gun was intended for general shooting of both game and other quarry. It incorporates John Manton's design for a flintlock breech patented in 1797.

This boar's head with pronounced snout on the trigger guard of a John Manton flintlock is an unusual decorative motif.

engraving is concerned, is that it had been used at a later date as a scrapbook in which Palmer pasted pulls of his engraving. Pulls are printed from examples of gun engraving using the intaglio method, in which ink is smeared into the engraving, the excess is wiped off, and then a piece of paper is impressed into the image using the pressure of the thumb.

Careful comparison of these pulls with extant examples of the Mantons' work has made it possible to identify guns engraved by Palmer. The engraver's general style, together with his treatment of dogs and game, allows us to say with a good degree of certainty that the Manton guns illustrated here were engraved by William Palmer.

The dogs in particular are definitive. Naive in style and apparently created from a series of circles and ellipses, in much the same way as one might teach a child to draw, a good example are a pair of silver percussion locks for a double-barreled sporting gun signed by Palmer with the mark "E. B." The initials probably signify Elizabeth Barnett, who recent scholarship suggests was the daughter or possibly the niece of Michael Barnett, a silversmith with strong connections to the gun trade. Incongruously, the locks bear the London hallmarks for 1827—which was after Palmer died—but the style is unmistakable, suggesting perhaps a son or an apprentice who had retained the house name.

Palmer also appears to have engraved guns for Alexander Forsyth, the famous minister of Belhelvie, Scotland, whose work with detonating powder helped usher in the percussion era. Pulls from the account books clearly show lockplates engraved with the name "Forsyth Patent."

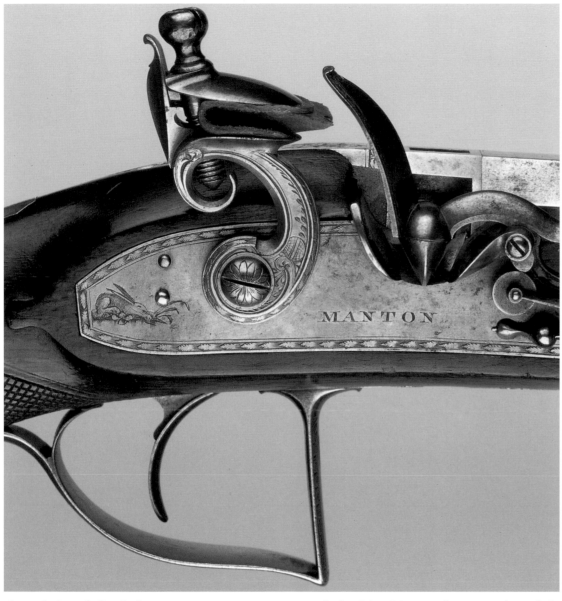

A single-barrel flintlock-sporting gun, circa 1812, made by John Manton for a member of the Egerton family, a 16-bore with 31-inch barrel. It is a classic example of a fully developed flintlock sporting gun by a best London maker when the overthrow of the flint ignition system by the percussion cap was still several years away.

One of Palmer's signature dogs on a John Manton single-flintlock gun. An almost identical image appears in the book of Palmer rubbings.

Palmer's birds appear to have a lot in common—stylistically—with his dogs

Another one of Palmer's signature houndlike dogs on the trigger guard of a Manton flintlock sporting gun.

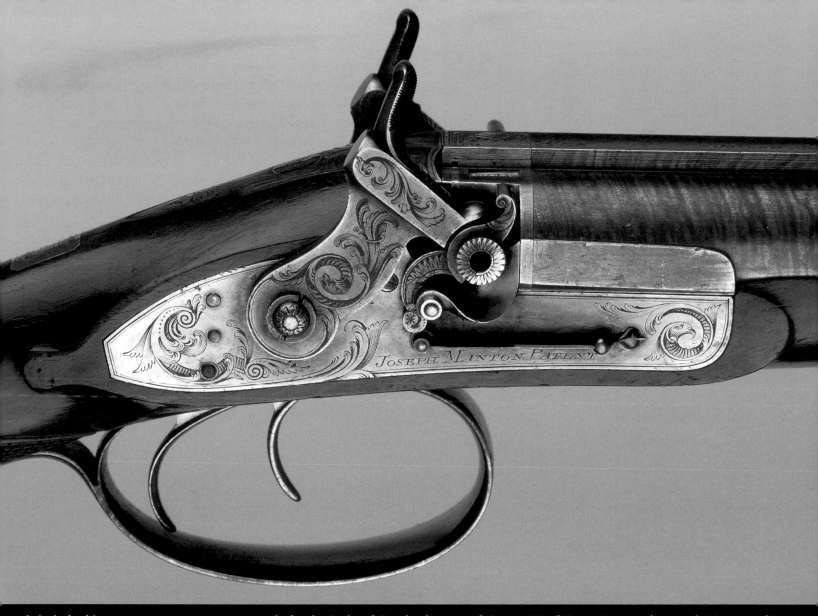

A tubelock double sporting gun, circa 1821, made for the Duke of Cambridge, son of George III of Great Britain, by Joseph Manton of Hanover Square, London. A 14-bore with 31-inch barrel, it was built on Joe Manton's second and successful percussion patent.

JOSEPH MANTON PATENT

Game-scene engraving on the John Manton single-flint fowler with patent breech.

Another Forsyth engraver was William Leykauff (or Leykauss) who, like Caslon, was a freeman of the association of loriners and who, like Palmer, engraved the copper plates used by printers. He engraved the plates from which the trade labels of Samuel Henry Staudenmayer, Richard Jackson, and Ambrose Fisher were printed, with his own signature, "Leykauss, Sculpt.," clearly visible in the bottom left-hand corner. In their book *Forsyth & Co.: Patent Gunmakers*, W. Keith Neal and D. H. L. Back record William Leykauff, of 4 Lisle Street, as an engraver who had "bills under acceptance" of £31-5-0 with Forsyth in 1809.

A man who stocked guns for both Joseph Manton and Forsyth & Co. was James Purdey; he eventually opened up his own gunmaking premises at 4 Princes Street off Leicester Square. He and Joe Manton appear to have constituted something of a mutual admiration society, and Richard Beaumont credits Purdey with the famous remark, "But for him we should have been a parcel of blacksmiths." Colonel Peter Hawker tells us that Manton said, "Purdey gets up the best work next to mine!"

Joseph Manton declared bankruptcy in 1826, only twelve years after Purdey opened his own business. James Purdey took over Manton's clientele. He became London's greatest gunmaker, employing Manton's last engraver, Peter Gumbrell.

Peter Gumbrell was an engraver of King Street, Golden Square, and a creditor of Joseph Manton's. He had worked for Joseph Manton at the same time that Purdey had worked for him, and he went unpaid at the time of Manton's bankruptcy. Purdey used Gumbrell extensively, and, as Pat Unsworth has pointed out in his excellent book *The Early Purdey's*, it is "hardly sur-

Piled arms with the Union flag in an oval as a central motif are a common theme in the Palmer book.

prising that the engraved sea serpents found on Manton's arms also figure on Purdey's early pieces." Gumbrell later moved to Marlborough Street, and Purdey was still using him as late as 1850.

At the time Gumbrell was engraving his last gun for Purdey, French pieces that loaded at the breech began to appear in England. Strengthened and anglicized, they would revolutionize sport shooting. The ease with which these new guns could be loaded helped to popularize shooting to the extent that traditional gun engravers could no longer meet the demand for their services. Decorative engravers were employed to fill the gap, bringing with them the bouquet and scroll formerly reserved for the backs of pocket watches.

It was a style introduced in London in the early 1870s by a Purdey engraver named Lucas, and it is still in use today. Its appeal is seemingly to lend immortality to a gun, and it is the only design that no one really appears to dislike. It's almost certainly the kind of work that J. F. Hayward was referring to in his introduction to *The Art of the Gunmaker 1660-1830* when he wrote: "I have myself visited an engraver of gunlocks in Soho up to a few years ago who used for the decoration of modern shot-guns patterns that dated back to the mid-nineteenth century."*

Although the extensive use of decorative engravers may have been new to London in the 1870s, in Birmingham the practice appears to have been established a century earlier—at least, that is, to judge from the recently rediscovered pattern book at the Victoria & Albert Museum. The reasons why Birmingham

The reference here may be to Harry Kell, or possibly Jack Sumner, who were both employing mid-nineteenth century engraving patterns and working in Soho at the time Hayward was writing this introduction.

gunmakers used decorative engravers while London did not become easier to understand when we learn that Birmingham did not have the deep traditions of book printing associated with London but instead had a long history of metalwork. Birmingham's jewelry quarter and gun quarter were, and still are, adjacent.

It is significant then that the only known English gun embellisher's pattern book is the work of a Birmingham man, Robert Wilson. Wilson was probably the gun finisher listed in contemporary directories as living on John Street (which was located across Steelhouse Lane from the gun quarter) and later on High Street, Bordesley.

While rare in England, pattern books for the design of weapons and armor were relatively common in continental Europe, but there is nothing to suggest that Wilson's work is anything but British. His scrolling foliage with flowers is archetypically English and could be the prototype for much that came later. His interlaced strapwork with stacked arms is just as visibly Scottish, and it may have been inspired by, or more likely intended for, all-metal pistols built in Birmingham in the Scottish style.

Several of Wilson's designs bear patriotic inscriptions such as "*Vivat Rex*," "Success to the British arms," and "Wilkes and liberty." This last refers not to the famous Beak Street gunmaker but to the notorious John Wilkes who belonged to the secret society known as the Hell-Fire Club, whose members held drunken orgies in a secret chapel adorned by an enormous sculpture of a phallus. Wilkes is largely forgotten today, but his suit against King George's minions for break-

Engraving on the breech of the Manton tubelock.

Too late for Palmer, this John Manton percussion double may be the work of William Leykauff, who is known from Coutts banking records to have engraved Manton guns. It is a double-barrel sporting gun, circa 1830, made for the fifth Earl of Oxford of Brampton Park, Herefordshire. A 17-bore with 30-inch barrels, it was built for game shooting by one of the leading London gunmakers originally founded by John Manton in 1781.

Engraving on the breech of a percussion gun by John Manton.

ing into his London house in 1763 so stirred the Sons of Liberty, who included John Adams and John Hancock, that they insisted that "the fate of Wilkes and America must stand or fall together." When the framers of the U.S. Constitution wrote the Fourth Amendment against "unreasonable searches and seizures" it was John Wilkes they had in mind. Wilkes eventually won his suit, and Americans celebrated by naming towns and children after him—from Wilkes-Barre, Pennsylvania, to John Wilkes Booth.

Other inscriptions refer to contemporary gunmakers such as "Richards" and "Thos. Gill, Birmingham." The former is probably Thomas or Theophilus Richards, while the latter is certainly Thomas Gill, a sword cutler and gunmaker of Jennens Row "near Bartholomew Chapel." Unfortunately, no extant weapons have yet to be linked with these original designs.

Today the tradition of employing engravers with backgrounds in the graphic arts (such as Geoffrey Caspard and Peter Cusack) or from the jewelry trades (Malcolm Appleby and Vincent Crowley, for example) continues. But the trend now is toward engravers whose entire careers are spent in the business of gun engraving.

The buttplate of a percussion gun by John Manton.

With engraving similar to that found on Forsyth guns, this Rigby, circa 1834, may be the work of Leykauff. (Photo: Tim Crawford)

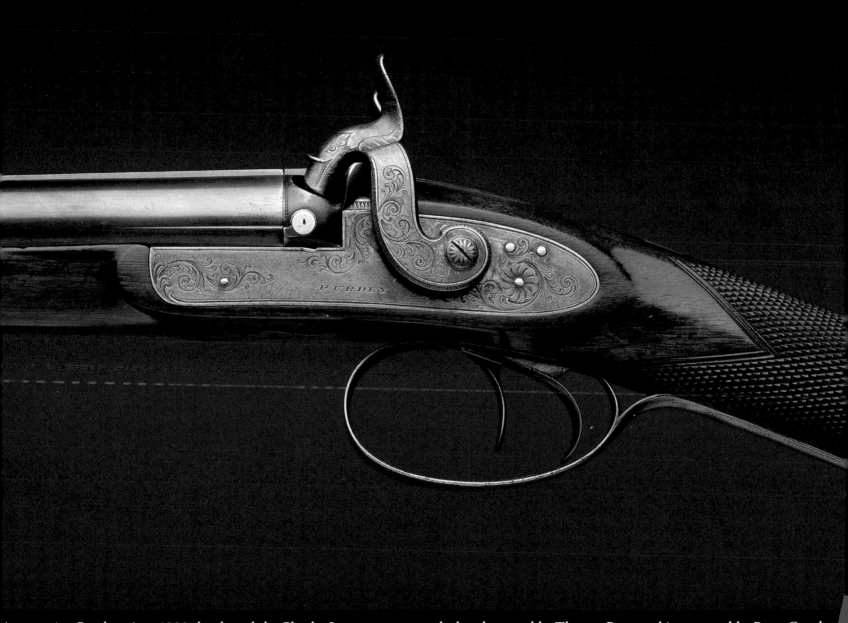

A percussion Purdey, circa 1829, has barrels by Charles Lancaster, was stocked and screwed by Thomas Boss, and is engraved by Peter Gumbrel.

This percussion Purdey with grip safety, serial number 1,322, was built in 1828 and is almost certainly the work of Peter Gumbrell. (Photo: Tim Crawford)

This Charles Lancaster flintlock was built for Sir Richard Sutton and was exhibited at the Great Exhibition of 1851.

Battling stags highlight the trigger guard of a percussion Charles Lancaster of 151 New Bond Street, London. It is a double rifle, circa 1853, built for Lord Bolton of Bolton Hall, Yorkshire.

The theme of red deer continues on the patch box of this Lancaster double rifle. A fine sporting rifle for deer-stalking in Scotland, rather than big-game shooting in Africa or India, it is of 40-bore with 30-inch barrels. The gun is sighted at 100, 200, and 300 yards and is rifled on the patented Lancaster smooth oval-bore system.

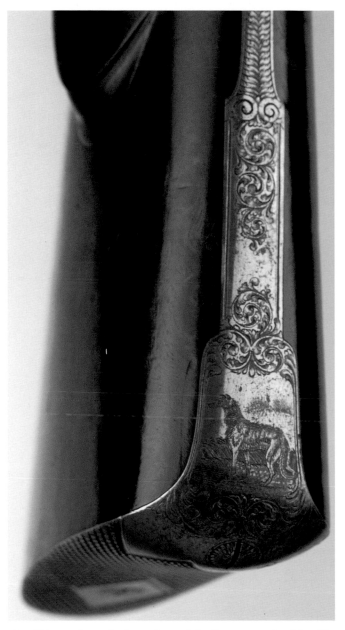

An elkhound on the buttplate of the Lancaster double rifle.

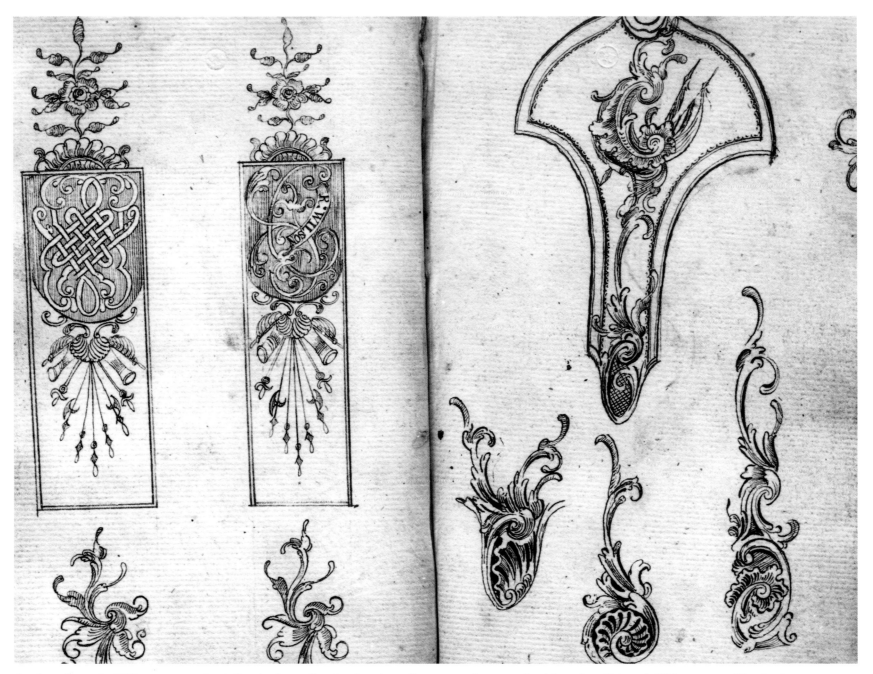

Designs from the Wilson pattern book for the butt of a pistol and small mounts plus two pistol barrels. Although Wilson was a Birmingham engraver, it is likely that the strapwork and piled-arms design on the left was intended for a Scottish pistol. (Photo: V. & A. Museum, London)

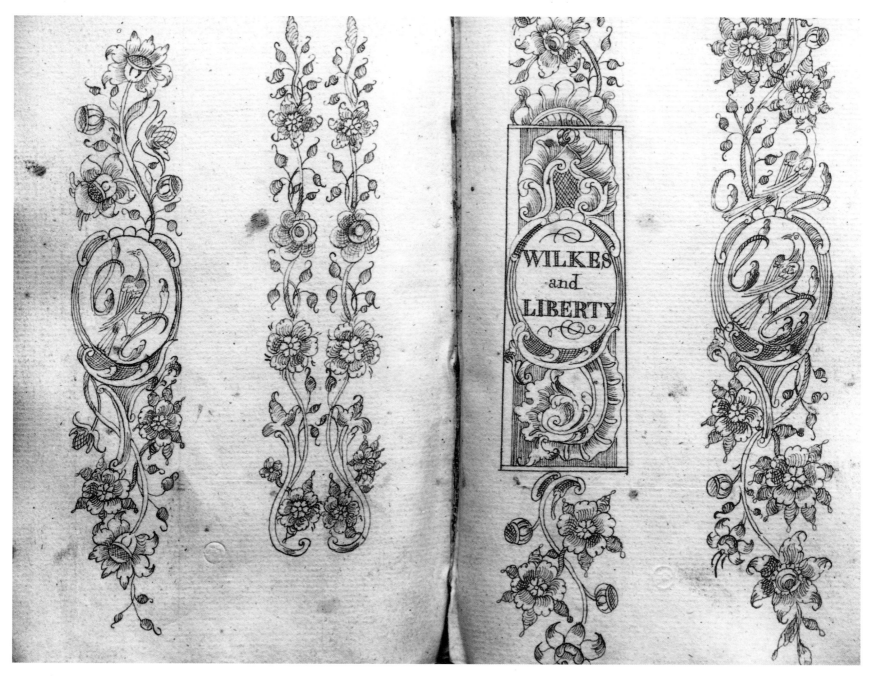

Four designs for gun barrels from the Robert Wilson pattern book in the Victoria and Albert Museum. (Photo: V. & A. Museum, London)

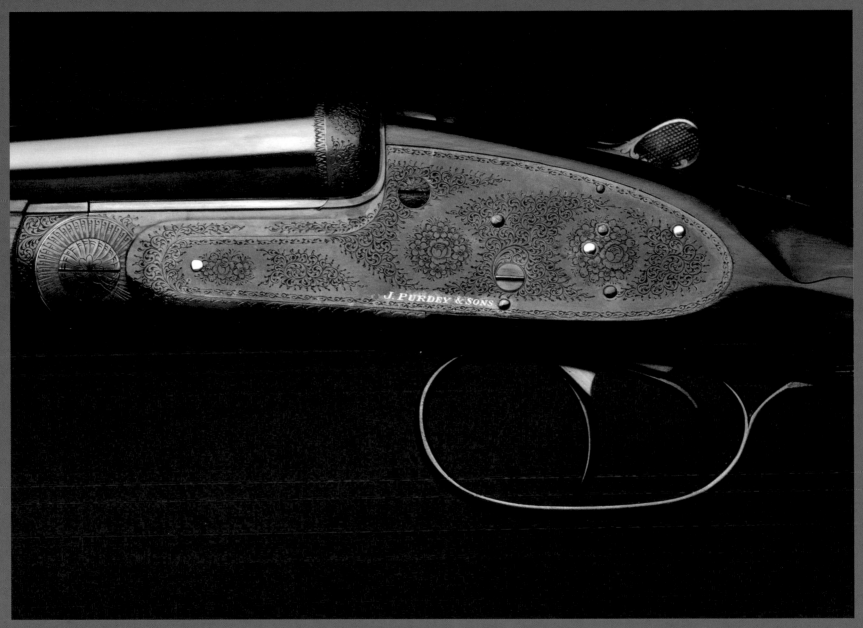

Purdey's standard bouquet and scroll as interpreted by Ken Hunt on a .410. More understated than those of their competitors, Purdey's bouquets resemble the lenses of a pair of asymmetrical spectacles.

Chapter 2

HOUSE STYLE

Imagine that you are an English gentleman of means living at the turn of the century, affluent but in a quandary. You require a pair of guns, but which guns?

Your duties in the Colonial Service may take you out to India. There, the opportunity for shooting driven chukar in Kashmir may present itself. You will be a long way from your gunmaker, so the guns you take must be sound and reliable. Because of your acquaintance with the Prince of Wales, you may be invited to shoot pheasants and partridge at Sandringham, so your guns should be fashionable and stylish. Who should make them?

A quarter of a century earlier, your choice might have been based on mechanical considerations. Makers then offered different patent actions, designed by themselves and developed in their own workshops. Every possible claim was made for the superiority of these mostly under-lever hammer guns, but by 1900 most of them were gone.

Hammer actions had been rendered obsolete. The standard design, which had grown from the hotbed of invention during the previous twenty-five years, had become a hybrid of the Purdey underbolt coupled to a Scott spindle and top-lever. It was a method of bolting guns so reliable that every maker employed it.

Quality too was not much help in making your decision. Every maker of best guns was a best amongst equals. If Boss introduced an assisted-opening gun, Purdey built one that was a self-opener. If Holland & Holland offered a rolled-edge trigger guard, Woodward countered with an articulated front trigger. By 1900, all four makers had incorporated each other's little niceties to the point where nothing of significance distinguished them. They all stood on the same high plateau of excellence.

At a time when all shotguns were side-by-side doubles—similar in the white and seemingly identical to the uninitiated even when finished—makers sought methods of making their guns look distinctive. This had become necessary because London makers all employed equivalent locks, which had developed from the same sources and were frequently made for the trade by the same makers in Darlston and Wolverhampton.

A Griffiths of Manchester with ducks, headlock plates, and wonderfully primitive game-scene engraving. (Photo: Michael Howarth)

This W. R. Pape features Newcastle hammers with graceful tapering curves that are rounded in cross-section but with their outer sides filed flat. (Photo: Sherman Bell)

The game rib, too, had been standardized, and most of the best makers offered some variant on the Southgate ejector. Style is what separated them, and it would be upon the basis of style that your decision would be made.

Communications between cities was difficult in the nineteenth century, and, as a consequence, different gun actions had developed in the relative isolation of the provinces. But just as important, distinctive regional styles developed in urban centres such as Newcastle and Manchester. Newcastle makers—Greener, Burnand, and Pape, for example—often used chamfered hammers with graceful tapering curves, rounded in cross-section but with their outer sides filed flat. Manchester makers such as Griffith and Gasquoine & Dyson frequently built lockplates that were in the shape of ducks' heads.

If, during the hammer gun era, stylistic devices had developed because provincial makers were isolated from each other's influence by distance, during the hammerless era such devices were employed in Edwardian London to distinguish gunmakers who worked only streets apart. In their efforts to pursue style, London's four best makers developed two distinct schools. Boss and Purdey gravitated toward a conservative, understated look directed toward a clientele that preferred not to see its family name printed in any context other than marriage or death. On the other hand, Woodward and Holland & Holland were both more ostentatious, attracting those with a more flamboyant lifestyle. The Boss pictured here is a fine example of the former, the Woodward the latter.

The ball fences on Boss guns were often beaded and engraved with bouquets of roses and fine scroll, while distinctive, deeply carved arcaded fences were synonymous with the Woodward name. The tumbler pivots on the Boss are flush with the lockplates and unobtrusive, while those on the Woodward protrude in an eye-catching manner. The treatment of the safeties is similar, Boss's being simplicity itself while Woodward's is of a T-shaped form with the bar of the T covering the word *Safe* in gold. Even the barrel length is a statement of style: Boss's barrels were frequently the standard 28 or 30 inches, while Woodward's were often made in an eccentric 29 inches.

It's odd that something as mundane as barrel length should have become a feature that makers used to display their individuality. But in addition to the Woodward 29-inch barrel, there were C. S. Rosson & Co. of Rampant Horse Street, Norwich, which will forever be associated with 27-inch barrels, and E. J. Churchill, a name inseparable from the 25-inch concept.

Boss and Purdey guns are often seen stocked with straight-grained wood, and Tom Purdey once accounted for the plain walnut on his firm's guns with this explanation: "The wood is only there to bring the actioned barrels to the shoulder." The Woodward philosophy regarding wood was just the opposite. Woodward stocks had a distinctive semipistol grip known as a "Woodward hand," cut from the most exotic walnut, of dramatic figure and contrast, imported from Circassia and the Dordogne.

The sole concession Boss made to anything less than conservative was to build guns with the action bodies rounded, perhaps to reduce weight, but in the process creating another stylistic feature that is today associated with their name. It was in their engraving styles,

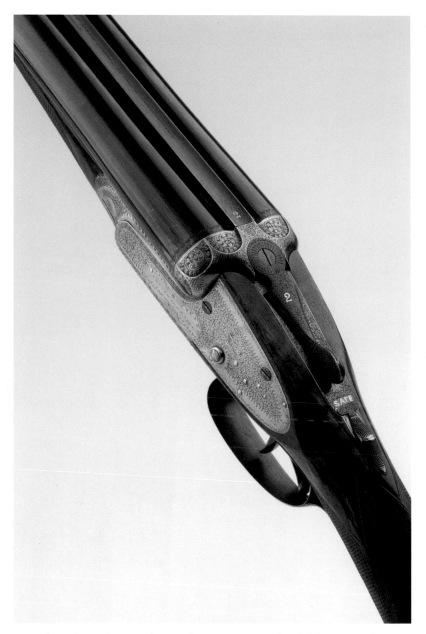

Woodward was known for its characteristic umbrellalike arcaded fences, T-shaped safety, protruding tumbler pivots, and a fine engraving style that featured the maker's name in a parchment on the bar of the action.

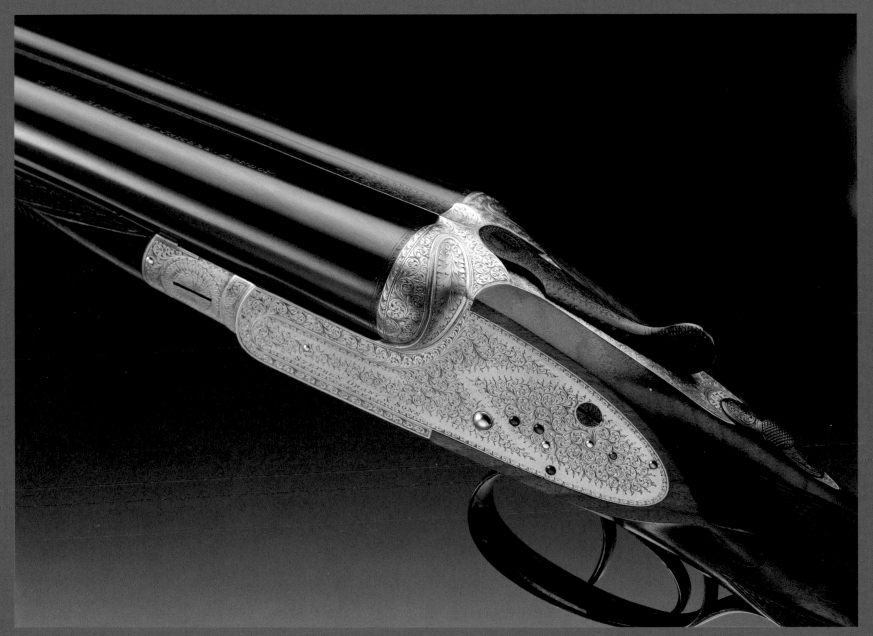

Stephen Grant had a house style as distinctive as that of any London maker, with fluted fences and two panels of scroll with a forward-facing chevron dividing them.

Boss engraving, like Purdey's featured bouquets of roses in a fine scroll background, but the difference was that as many as seven asymmetrical bouquets were on the lockplate and fences. This example is the rare three-barreled model and is almost certainly the work of Jack Sumner.

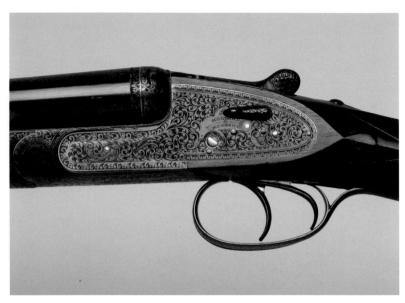

These Holland & Holland house engravings feature bold, open foliate scrolls, descended from an acanthus motif.

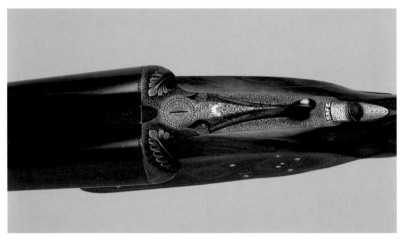

Occasionally elements from one gunmaker's house style will appear on another's gun. An example of this is these fluted fences—a design motif of Stephen Grant— seen here on Purdey. Bespoke gunmakers will change their style on request.

however, that builders of the London best guns most distinctively expressed their individuality. Woodward opted for a fine parchment scroll with the maker's name on the bar. Holland & Holland delighted in a foliate scroll based on an acanthus leaf, borrowed from the Arts and Crafts movement. Purdey and Boss both used bouquets of roses in a fine scroll background, which, while ostensibly similar, are actually very different. Purdey bouquets resemble a pair of spectacle lenses of two different sizes, a design widely copied, particularly by Spanish gunmakers. Boss on the other hand employed as many as seven asymmetrical bouquets widely distributed across the lockplate, frame, and fences.

One common misconception about bouquet and scroll is that—although a signature of London guns— one maker's style was indistinguishable from that of the next. That is not true, and the following example is offered for clarification. A well-known writer with a London best gun engraved with bouquet and scroll did not know who had made his gun, because the name had been tampered with. An enthusiast of British guns happened to hear of the mystery and immediately recognized the engraving style of the maker. The firm had long since gone out of business, but fortunately the maker's records are extant. The writer was pleasantly surprised to find his pride and joy among them. Mystery solved!

It is slightly ironic that in a bespoke gun trade—in which every gun is made to a particular customer's specifications—house style should be so pervasive. Of course features associated with one maker will occasionally turn

Single barreled .246.

Over and under by Kent Hill.

Over and under by Brad Tallet.

As well as offering bouquet and scroll—referred to as "standard fine" in catalogues and included in the basic price of the gun—Purdey also offered something they called "extra finish" at an additional cost. Here are three examples as interpreted by three generations of Purdey engravers. The first is a single-barreled rifle in .246 (2 1/4), a Purdey proprietary cartridge, attributed to Harry Kell, circa 1928. The second is an over-and-under by Ken Hunt, circa 1968, and the third, also an over-and-under, is a recent gun by Brad Tallett.

up on a gun made by another, but that is usually in the case of special orders. A customer might commission a Purdey with a Boss-style rounded body or a Holland & Holland with Woodward protruding tumbler pivots—but these are exceptions rather than the rule.

Ultimately, your decision in choosing a pair of guns would have been based on which house style most closely suited your taste, and taste is personal. Whatever your choice, it would likely have outlived you. Long after you turned to dust, your guns would have suffered the curse of immortality. Today, one hundred years later, as the next century turns, someone faced with a similar dilemma will perhaps see these guns. Once again, someone affluent enough to pursue driven shooting—red legs in Spain or gray partridge on the Hungarian plains, grouse in Scotland or pheasants in the Czech Republic—will carry them home. If the guns are bought from a reputable dealer or an established auction house they will still function perfectly, and the new owner will have the satisfaction of having shared a taste in house style.

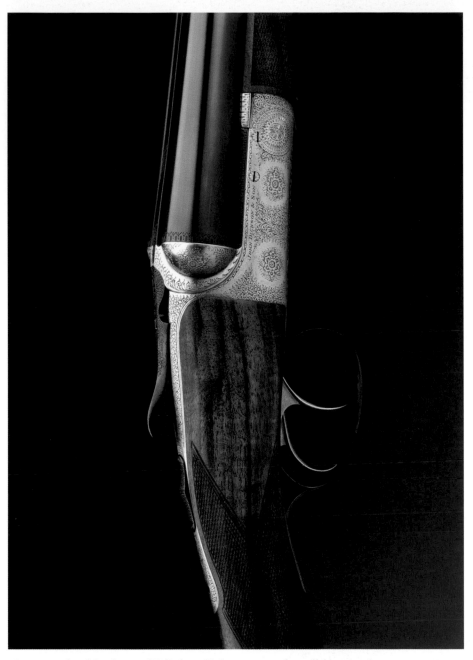

An example of Dickson of Edinburgh's bouquet and scroll house style.

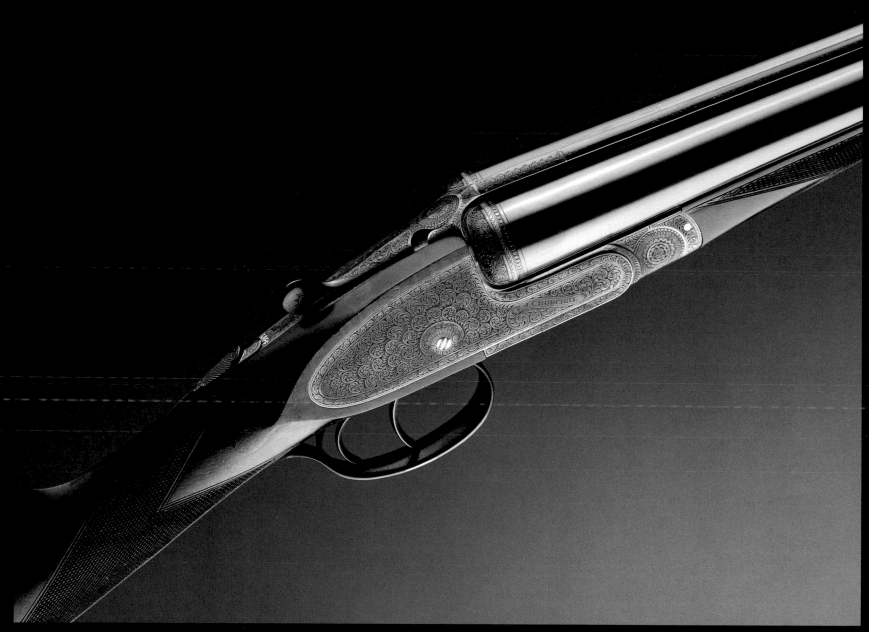

Churchill's standard pattern features pinless locks and close scrollwork emanating outward from the tumbler pivot.

Opposite page: Boss-style bouquet and scroll engraving on this, the only round-bodied Boss over-and-under they ever built.

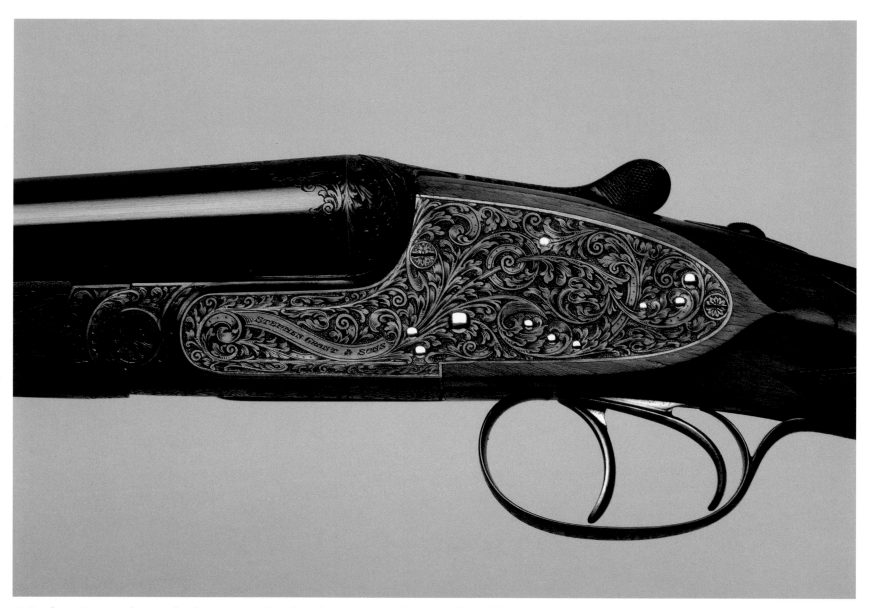

A Stephan Grant with extra finish engraving thought to have originated in the Kell workshop.

Chapter 3

HARRY KELL

Game animals so captivate the human imagination that we have been depicting them since Paleolithic times. Deer and bison were common images on the walls of caves occupied by our ancestors, and the cave paintings in the Dordogne region of France and in northern Spain, dating from 13,000 to 14,000 years ago, also include depictions of wildfowl.

Some think that by making an image of game, early man believed that he could bring the animals within his grasp. Long after such superstitions died out, however, the tradition of depicting animals of the chase continued to thrive. Nowhere is that more obvious than on weaponry.

Spears and swords used in medieval Europe in pursuit of wild boar were often decorated with elaborately engraved hunting scenes. No sooner were firearms developed than they too were similarly embellished. The heavily decorated gun reached its decadent apogee during the late eighteenth century, with some of the most lavishly finished being made by Boutet of Versailles.

In Britain the level of decoration popular on the Continent was seen as ostentatious, and a more conservative style was adopted. Starting with the open scroll during Georgian times, British gunmakers progressed to acanthus leaf and fruiting vine motifs. Such classical aesthetic allusions suggested gravity and dignity, and fostered the illusion that Western civilization had descended in one unbroken tradition from Elysium to Elveden. Game-scene engraving, where it did occur, tended to be naive both in content and execution. I recently had the opportunity to handle a lovely old J. D. Dougall muzzleloader that was completely covered with fruiting vine engraving, the patch box being engraved with a lion and a tiger that stared out at the viewer with the benignity of animals from a child's nursery.

Throughout its history, game-scene engraving has tended to shadow popular mainstream art. Early examples such as the Dougall patch box tend to look like the paintings of George Stubbs. In the Victorian era, engravers such as G. E. Lewis unashamedly borrowed from Sir Edward Landseer, and in the early twentieth century the best engravers found their inspiration in the works of Archibald Thorburn and J. C. Harrison.

The difficulty in transposing Thorburn into steel was compounded by the animated nature of Edwardian wildlife art.

Whereas the paintings of Stubbs and, to a lesser extent, Landseer depict stationary, flat animals, Thorburn's birds are alive and in flight.

Few men were capable of capturing movement on the small area of a lockplate. The very best of those who could was Harry Kell. Born in 1880 into a family of coppersmiths and engravers, he was indentured as an engraving apprentice with the firm of Sanders and Kell at the age of fourteen and became a journeyman around 1900. When Thomas Sanders died in 1919, Henry John Kell took his son Harry into partnership with him. When the old man died in 1928, Harry became his own boss.

Working freelance from a succession of addresses on the wrong side of Regent Street, Harry engraved guns for the West End's most prestigious gunmakers. Purdey, Woodward, Holland & Holland, and Boss all beat a path to his door. When he died in 1958, he was considered the finest engraver of his time, employing a workforce capable of producing any of the numerous scroll patterns we associate with the makers of London's best guns. But, more important, he was also responsible for breathing life into game-scene engraving, thereby providing a bridge between the naive game-scene engravers of the nineteenth century and the rigorous realists of our own age.

Unfortunately, Harry Kell signed only a tiny percentage of his work, so knowing which guns are Kell-engraved and which are not is difficult. The problem is compounded because Kell trained a stable of engravers who used his pattern books and worked for him in his Soho workshops. This "school of Kell" engraving is encountered fairly frequently, but it is more often than not the work of an unknown hand in the studio of the master, possibly working under his supervision.

Harry Kell at work on a Dickson round action in the early 1950s. (Photo: Hunt/Trevallion)

The senior Harry Kell, who died in 1928. (Photo: Hunt/Trevallion)

The engraved brass plaque from the door of Kell's Soho workshop.

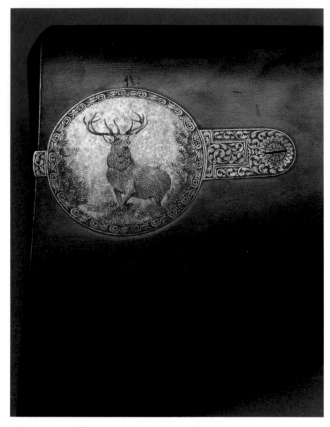

The patch box of this Alexander Henry gun, serial number 555, circa 1860, is the work of an unknown engraver. In keeping with many of the Edinburgh-built guns, the game scene here is remarkably sophisticated. The image is clearly based on Sir Edward Landseer's "Monarch of the Glen," perhaps the most widely reproduced image of the Victorian era.

The nursery tiger on the trigger guard of this muzzleloader is typical of game scenes before Kell. Although well executed, it was clearly the work of someone who had never seen the man-killers of India. The model was probably the engraver's house cat.

Gray, or English, partridge on the action of a boxlock by G. E. Lewis. When Lewis died in 1917, his obituary read in part: "He also cultivated his artistic faculty by attendance in the evening at an art school. There are still preserved a number of the reductions of hunting scenes by Landseer and other artists, made by him for adaptation to the engraving of gunlocks in which he became an expert." (Photo: Sherman Bell)

A W. & C. Scott gun from the 1870s. The shorebirds, ducks, and geese on Scott guns of this era are highly naturalistic as though executed by a keen observer of live birds. These images appear to have been inspired by the great scientific bird books from the golden age of lithography—Gould, Lear, and Joseph Wolf. They may be the work of James Charles Scott, who worked as an engraver before becoming a partner. (Photo: Sherman Bell)

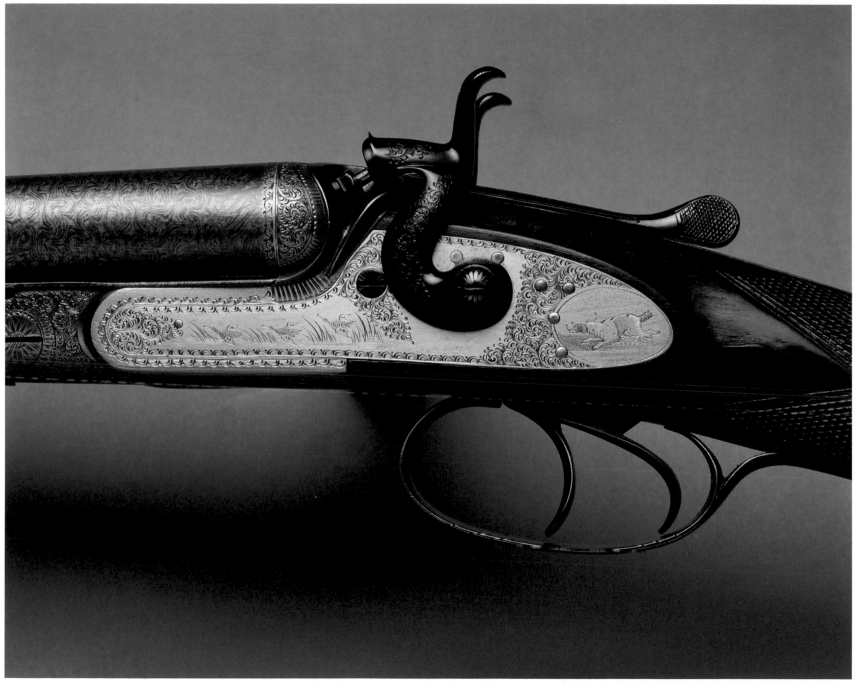

Typical bog standard game scene engraving before Harry kell with crude dog in cartouche at the back of the lock plate chasing snipe that look like sparrows smoking cigarettes.

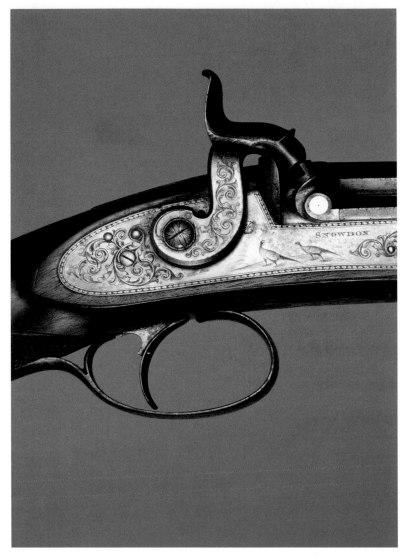

The pheasants on this George Snowdon of Alnwick, Northumberland, were typical of the naive nature of game-scene engraving before Harry Kell. The unknown engraver may have toiled away in a Newcastle workshop, seeing only those birds hanging in game dealers' windows. (Photo: Tim Crawford)

What little we do know about Kell comes from gunmakers' records and the sketch and pattern books he presented to his daughter-in-law, Lorna B. Kell, in June of 1958. While gunmakers' records are fairly sparse, we do know that Kell engraved the miniature Purdey's for H. M. the Queen's dollhouse and the pair presented to King George V on the occasion of his Silver Jubilee. The pattern books, which were sold at Christie's in November 1994 for £3,450, are perhaps the greatest treasury of information on Kell. They include an image of a backlock gun engraved in an oriental manner for the king of Siam in 1912, photos of a deeply carved gun with griffins and putti in the style of Barre of Paris, and rubbings of a "Centenary year" Dickson with a vignette of Princes Street among bold scrolling foliage. Various house styles are also represented by the close scroll we associate today with Churchill guns and its antithesis, the bold, open, deeply cut engraving synonymous with Watson brothers. However, game scenes dominate the book. Of the fifteen plates illustrated in the Christie's catalogue, more than half show animals of the chase.

Apart from the tendency toward game-scene engraving and the obvious quality of the work, the overall impression is one of diversity. Although Kell and his school may have favored game scenes, they were clearly capable of any style of engraving. A good example is the gun in the style of Aristide Barre.

It appears that the original gun in this style was built by Purdey for the shah of Iran in 1892 and engraved by Barre. A second, in identical style, was built around 1911, and when a third was needed to match it in the mid-twenties, Purdey's were faced with a dilemma because Barre had died in 1922. Harry Kell apparently stepped in and perfectly

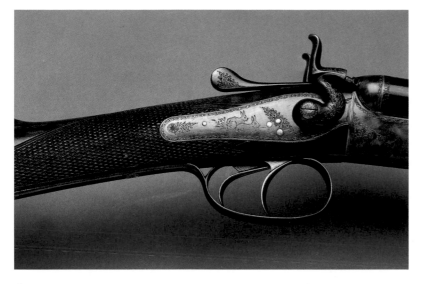

a.

b.

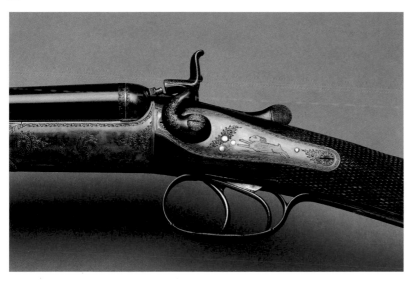

c.

d.

Typical of game-scene engraving before Kell, this novel sequence illustrates a narrative in scenes: (a) at rest; (b) alert; (c) running; (d) bowled over. The gun is a Cogswell & Harrison .410. Contemporary Coggie documents refer to this type of weapon as "specially recommended for ornithologists collecting specimens and killing of medium- and small-sized birds, vermin, and such like."

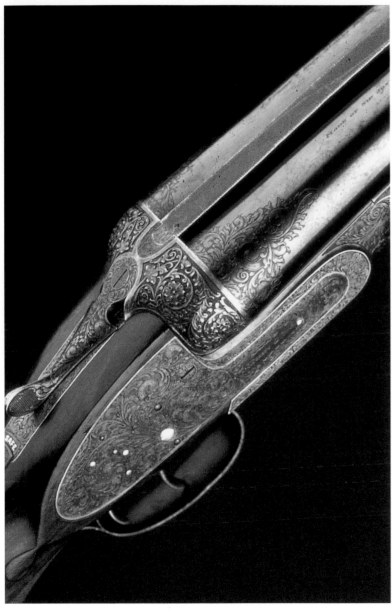

An exceptional James Purdey 8-bore built in 1923. Although the Purdey records make no mention of an engraver, the engraving is thought to be the work of Harry Kell. (Photo: Bonhams)

duplicated the style of the earlier guns, adopting Barre's engraving techniques in the process.

Harry Kell died in 1958, but his mantle is worn today by the man he trained, the world-renowned engraver Ken Hunt. His work, although obviously inspired by Kell's, has taken its own direction. In one important way, though, Ken Hunt's engraving maintains a Kell tradition: His cuts are deep, crisp, and clean. Hunt's engraving, much like Kell's—and unlike banknote engraving—will last many lifetimes. In another respect Ken's engraving both differs from and parallels Kell's. Like the work of engravers before him, Ken's work reflects the popular wildlife artists of his day. Today much of wildlife art is in the hyper-realistic style made popular in the 1970s, and Ken Hunt's engraving frequently shows that influence.

Before Kell, English engravers did not normally sign their work; they were simply anonymous artisans. Today, because of Kell, the best engravers have been rightly elevated to the stature of artists who, like others, take full credit for, and sign, their work. Before Kell, game-scene engraving was naive and lifeless. Today, because of his influence, game scenes are realistic and vibrant. Looking back over Kell's career, we see the body of work of a valued artist. But his engraved guns and working sketches are only a part of his legacy. His real significance continues to be the changes that sprang from his talent.

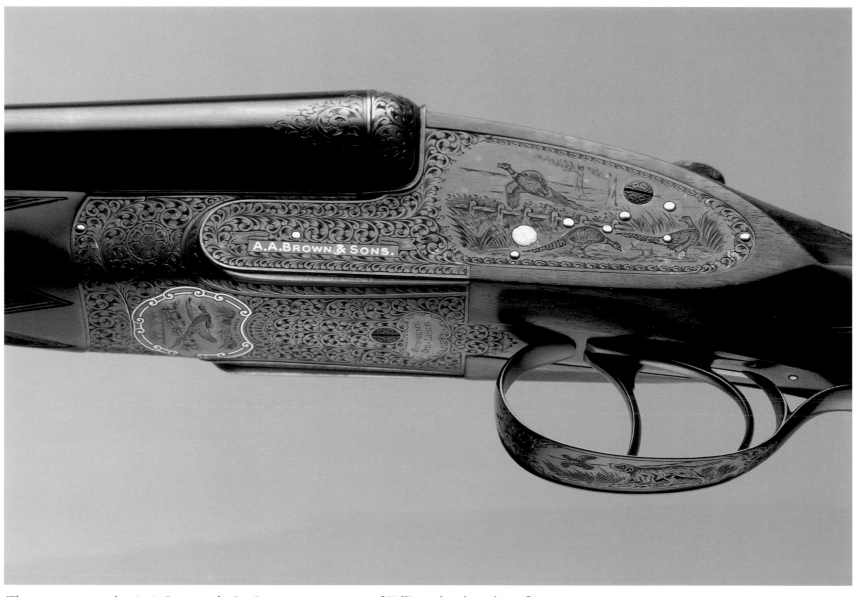

The game scene on this A. A. Brown is by Les Jones, a contemporary of Kell's, and it shows his influence.

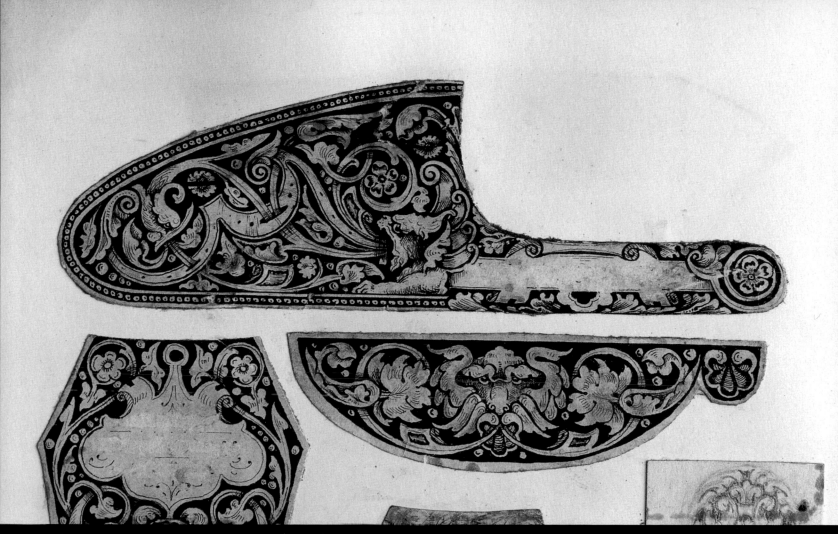

Rubbings from an unmarked gun that Kell engraved with pierced strapwork, bold foliate scroll, and exotic beasts.

Opposite page: The Kell legacy can be seen on this single-barrel trap gun by Boss. Engraved by Ken Hunt, who served his apprenticeship with Harry Kell, it should be compared with illustrations on this page and page 57 to see how similar design elements have been refined to produce an altogether more sophisticated result.

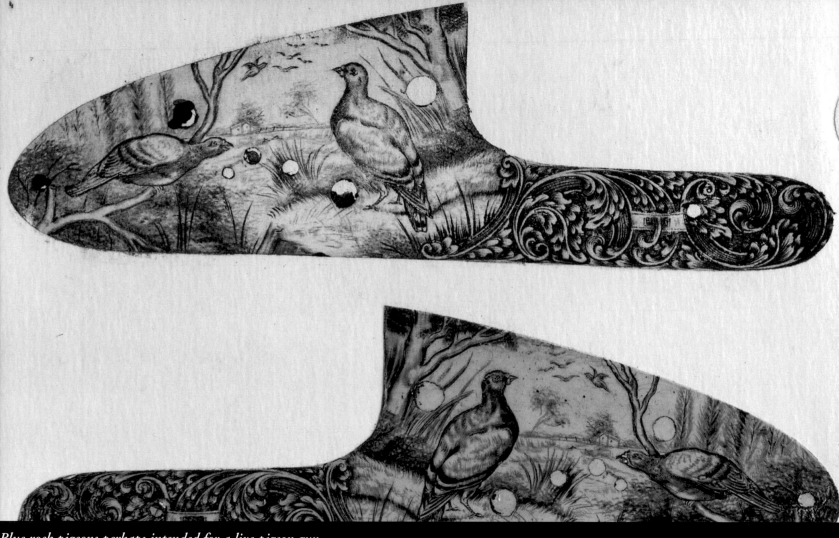

Blue rock pigeons perhaps intended for a live pigeon gun.

The ducks here are inspired by the paintings of Archibald Thorburn. The manner in which Thorburn exaggerated key elements of a bird's anatomy—in this case the mandibles—made his work ideal for transfer to a small lockplate. Few engravers, however, had the ability in Kell's day to capture the animated nature of Thorburn's work. The grass and/or rushes bleeding to the edge of the lockplate are a signature Kell element.

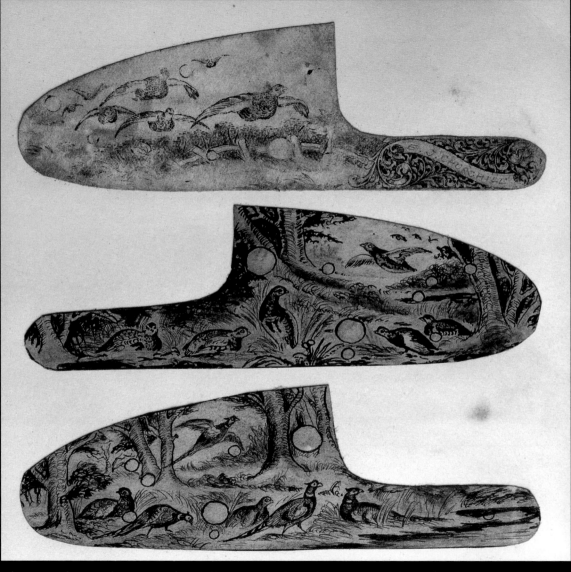

The partridge on this E. J. Churchill appear to have been inspired by such Thorburn paintings as "swerving from the gun."

Compare the pheasants on this J. Purdey & Sons to the work on the later A. A. Brown by Les Jones (Page 49). The similarities—particularly with regard to the attenuated bodies—are obvious.

The stags on this lockplate suggest that it may have been intended for a double rifle. The game scene running to the edge of the locks, without the benefit of a border, is typical of much of Kell's work.

The scrolling foliage on this flat-back action lock is all the more dramatic for the hatched matte ground.

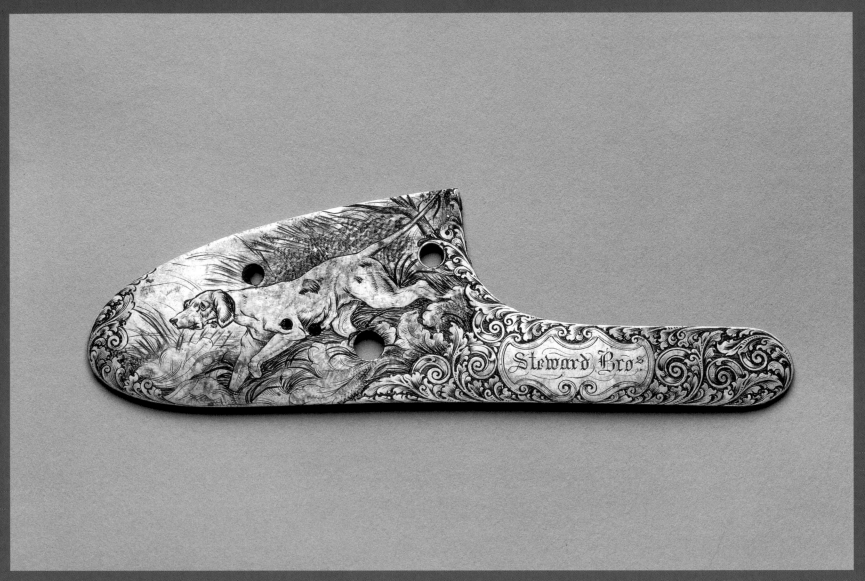

The manner in which the dog's muscles have been rendered by crosshatching suggests an aesthetic sophistication not seen in Kell's contemporary rivals.

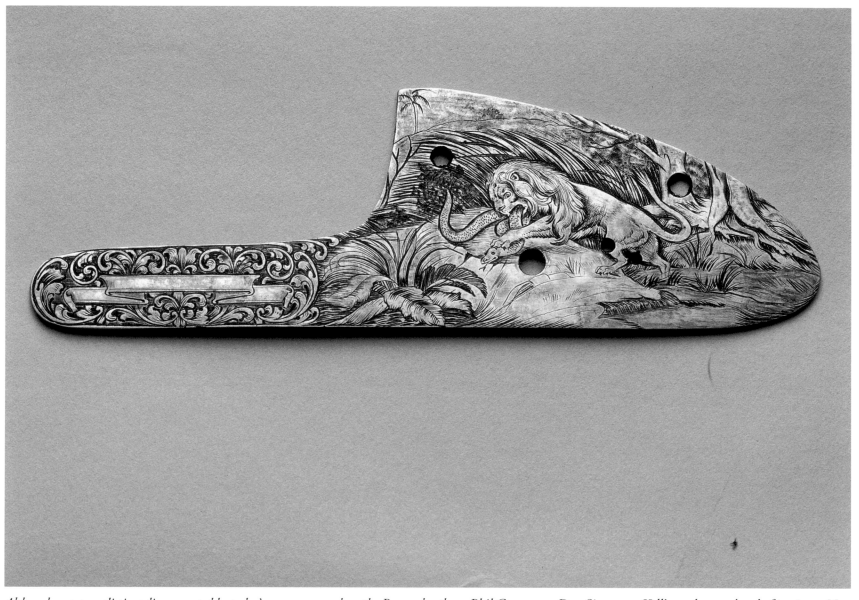

Although not as realistic as lions created by today's engravers, such as the Brown brothers, Phil Coggan, or Don Simmons, Kell's work was ahead of its time. Note the game scene running to the edge of the lockplate.

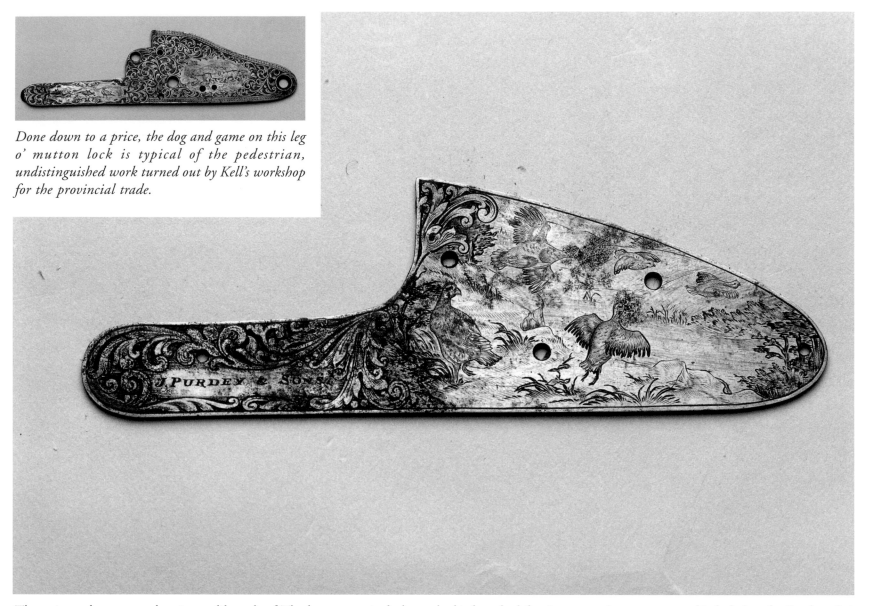

Done down to a price, the dog and game on this leg o' mutton lock is typical of the pedestrian, undistinguished work turned out by Kell's workshop for the provincial trade.

The animated nature and caricaturelike style of Thorburn—particularly on the bird at the left—is once again apparent on this lockplate for Purdey. It is atypical in having a lined border.

A selection of floor plates from the Kell workshop.

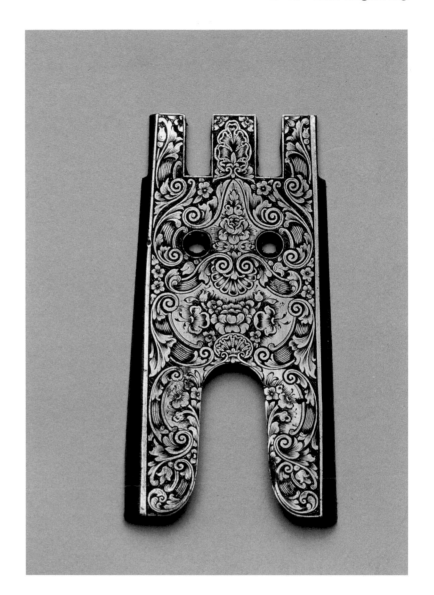

More floor plates from the Kell workshop.

Attributed to Kell are this pair of sidelever 12/20's by Stephan Grant.

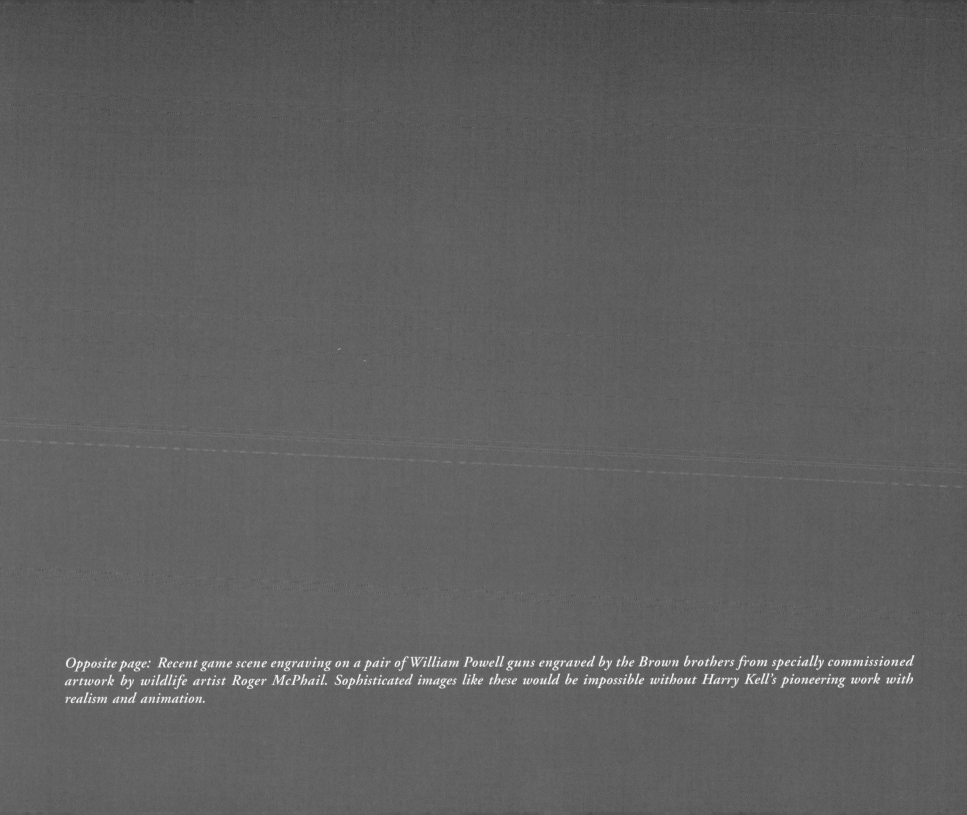

Opposite page: Recent game scene engraving on a pair of William Powell guns engraved by the Brown brothers from specially commissioned artwork by wildlife artist Roger McPhail. Sophisticated images like these would be impossible without Harry Kell's pioneering work with realism and animation.

An over-and-under by George Gibbs with Celtic strapwork by Don Simmons. The Celtic theme has been extended to the wrist and forearm, where strapwork replaces the more conventional chequering.

Chapter 4

CELTIC ENGRAVING

A gun's appeal can be understood on several levels: For some it is simply a tool, for others "history you can touch." But the person in search of a better mousetrap or the physical manifestation of a period of time often misses the point: A gun's strongest appeal is almost always aesthetic.

The British best gun in many ways embodies the Bauhaus ideal that "form follows function." Best guns have evolved over a long period of time to do a specific job, a job they do extraordinarily well. As a consequence they exhibit a grace of line not seen in weapons designed from scratch. But in one important way they also differ from Bauhaus philosophy, and that is in the area of engraving. Whereas Bauhaus design would

have perceived engraving as superfluous—gilding the lily—we think of it as an extension of the gun's aesthetic appeal.

Major Sir Gerald Burrard once attempted to justify engraving on the grounds of function, arguing "in the course of time, when the color of the final case-hardened parts wears off . . . the side-plates and action would flicker in the sun almost like a heliograph. . . . The engraving breaks up this surface and, further, has the effect of hiding the screw heads." But that is the view of a too-practical mind, and most of us would agree that the point of engraving is to raise the aesthetic appeal of an already beautiful piece of work.

Engraving also helps give a gun character, and even identity. Anyone with

sufficient knowledge can look at a gun chased with oak leaves and scenes of wild boar carved in deep relief and tell you that it's German. Bouquet and scroll, on the other hand, is the signature of London's makers and their imitators, and Celtic engraving is almost entirely, but not exclusively, the product of Scottish gunmakers.

That, however, has not always been the case. Until the mid-Victorian period Scottish shotguns looked a lot like English shotguns, with scroll and game scenes being the most popular designs. This began to change in 1852, when Queen Victoria and Prince Albert bought Balmoral, a castle and estate in the Dee Valley. Soon wealthy financiers and industrialists were following the royal example and taking the newly completed railway north to buy stalking privileges and shooting rights to Scotland's deer forests and grouse moors. This occurred at the height of the Empire, and the new visitors brought with them an imperial view of Scotland as "Scotlandshire" or "North Britain," rather than as a separate country with its own culture and traditions. Needless to say, there was a strong Scottish reaction, and artisans sought for forms of expression that would allow them to assert their national identity, or "Scottishness."

In 1890 Alexander Henry, the famous Edinburgh gunmaker, built a double rifle for Her Majesty Queen Victoria. Although Henry gave his address as "NB"—or North Briton—in his advertisements, the gun was tastefully finished in Celtic tendril or vine-scroll engraving. The gun, which is now in the royal gun room at Sandringham, is an early expression of what has come to be known as the Romantic Revival in Scotland.

These romantic revivals seem to occur in waves whenever Scottish identity is threatened by the encroaching English. The first of these revivals was triggered when Sir Walter Scott played host to a royal visit from George IV in 1822. Yet another appears to be under way as I write, to judge by the number of Scottish gunmakers, such as Daniel Fraser, who are once again engraving their guns in Celtic style. It is no coincidence that this is taking place at a time of renewed interest in Scottish nationalism.

The origins of Celtic art are lost in antiquity, but the reason why this style of decoration was adopted by Scottish gunmakers is easily understood. The Celts arrived in Britain from Europe between 400 and 100 B.C., bringing their distinctive style of ornamentation with them. These people became the ancient Britons, who fought so well

A top-lever hammer gun by W. R. Pape of Newcastle engraved in Celtic tendril or vine scroll, and similar in style to the guns offered by Hubert W. Paton of Perth. The vine scroll shown here is almost identical to that on the late seventh-century Bewcastle cross, which is located close to the Northumbrian border in Cumbria in an area that was familiar to William Rochester Pape. (Photo: Sherman Bell)

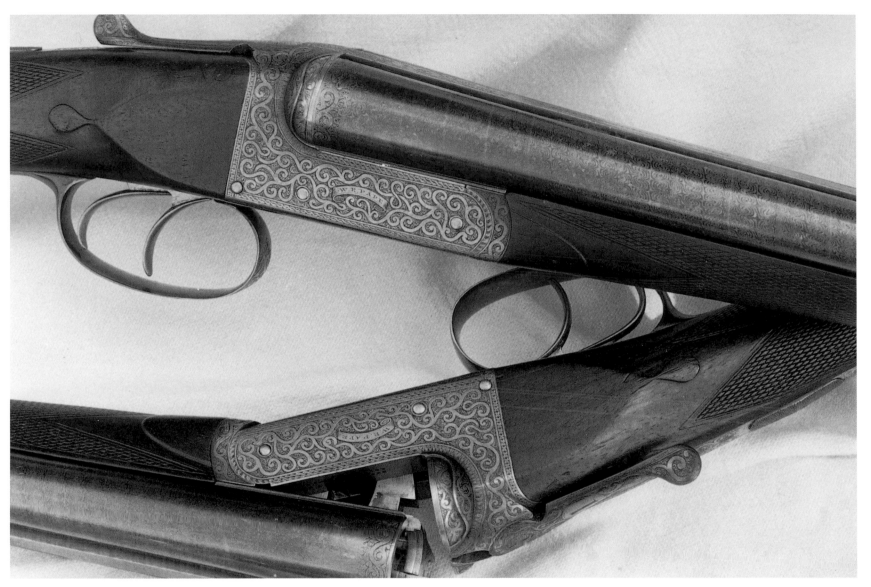

A pair of best boxlock ejectors with Celtic tendril or vine-scroll engraving, an appropriate choice for a weapon because it was a design found on fine Celtic swords discovered in La Tene in Switzerland. The guns are by W. R. Pape of Newcastle-upon-Tyne, who was not a Scottish maker but who lived and worked in the border country, an area with strong connections to Celtic art. (Photo: Fredrik Franzen)

This Holland & Holland sporting clays over-and-under is engraved in a style inspired by Doune pistols, with stacked trophies of tam-o'-shanter, bagpipes, harp, targe, battle-ax, skean dhu, and basket-hilt claymore. Celtic knotwork borders and thistles engraved to the bolster complement the Scottish theme. John Salt is the engraver.

The Scottish theme continues on this trigger plate-action gun with a vignette of a red grouse in highland landscape.

against Julius Caesar and successive waves of Roman conquest. After the Romans withdrew, the Picts, the Scots, and other Celtic tribes dominated Britain. Then, in the middle of the fifth century, the "English," or "Angles," together with their Saxon allies, invaded Britain from what is now Germany. The Celtic Britons were forced north and west onto the unproductive lands of what has come to be known as the Celtic Fringe—Ireland, Wales, and Scotland—where their descendants survive to this day, speaking various forms of the old Celtic language, Gaelic. So it is hardly surprising that Scottish gunmakers, looking back through their history and searching for some essential difference between themselves and their powerful neighbors, should have been attracted to Celtic design.

In the eighteenth century, distinctive highland pistols with iron stocks and rams' horn butts, made in the town of Doune by Caddell, Murdoch, Campbell, or Christie, were occasionally engraved with a loose strapwork inspired by Celtic designs. Degenerate forms of these pistols made by Birmingham makers such as Greener were often worn as costume accessories during the Victorian era.

The earliest examples of Celtic-engraved, breechloading shotguns were hammer guns by makers such as Edward Paton & Son of Perth and Daniel Fraser of 4 Leith Street Terrace, Edinburgh. In 1884, Fraser published an advertisement which read: "Attention is solicited to our new pattern of engraving, after pure Celtic designs, by Hubert W. Paton, Esq. This style of ornament is extremely handsome, and is admirably adapted for the decoration of high class Guns and Rifles intended for presentation."

It's tempting to think that Hubert Paton may have been the son of Edward Paton. These guns, which date from the late Victorian era, are very often found with Celtic tendril

The ancient Celts found a highly stylized rendering of the triskelion motif ideal for filling corners and circles.

or vine-scroll engraving. It is an appropriate form of decoration for a weapon, as it is often seen on ancient Celtic swords, particularly those found at La Tene in Switzerland. This initial wave of Celtic gun engraving found its inspiration in the great archeological finds of rare Celtic treasures, such as the Tara Brooch and the Ardagh Chalice, discovered in Ireland in the 1850s and 1860s.

Another generation of Celtic guns appeared between the two world wars—a period many consider to be the highwater mark of British gunmaking—and bore the names of such makers as Alex Martin of Glasgow, John McPherson of Inverness, and, again, Alexander Henry of Edinburgh. These guns were sidelocks, and, humorously enough, they all appear to have been made and engraved in Birmingham by Webley and Scott. They typically have a motif of knotwork or interlaced strapwork inspired by illuminated manuscripts such as the Lindisfarne Gospels and the Book of Kells, as interpreted by designers such as Archibald Knox.

Ironically, Celtic engraving is not well adapted to the traditional Scottish round action guns built by James McNaughton and John Dickson. Dicksons never built a gun with Celtic engraving because they understood that the flat ribbon motif required the flat surfaces of a sidelock or boxlock to show to best advantage. McNaughton, on the other hand, built several, and one that I have seen, built for the marquis of Bute in 1915, exemplified the problem. Even though the actioner had attempted to square off the action body to provide a flatter canvas, the engraving looked like a ball of twine unraveling. English guns with Celtic engraving are rare, though William Rochester Pape of Newcastle-upon-Tyne made many. Pape shot regularly in the borders and was no doubt familiar with the Lindisfarne Gospels; that is perhaps why boxlock Papes with vine-scroll engraving are relatively common. James Woodward of St. James Street, London, built at least one garniture of three Celtic-style guns, but these were probably a special order for a Scottish or Irish nobleman. In recent years Holland & Holland, a firm with no obvious Scottish connection, have built several Celtic guns. But Holland & Holland have a practice of decorating their guns in the tradition of the Arts and Crafts movement, that being the obvious source of their Celtic style.

Today, the demand created by people of Scottish descent worldwide has ensured that Celtic-style guns will always fetch a high price in the second-hand market. You can, of course, always have your new bespoke gun engraved in the manner of the Celts, but the high price and a certain Scottish thriftiness mean that it's less and less likely to happen.

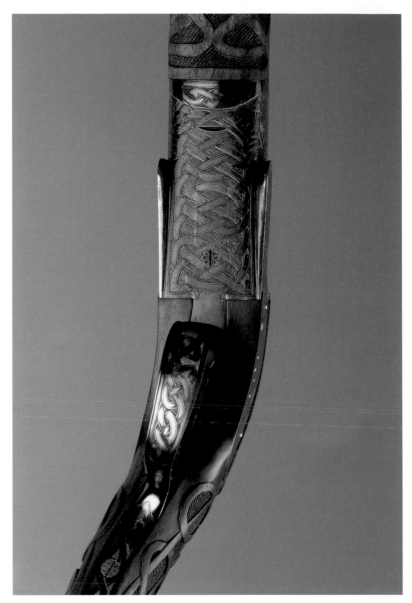

Besides unconventional strapwork at the wrist and forearm, this George Gibbs has a crossover stock for a right-handed person with a dominant left eye.

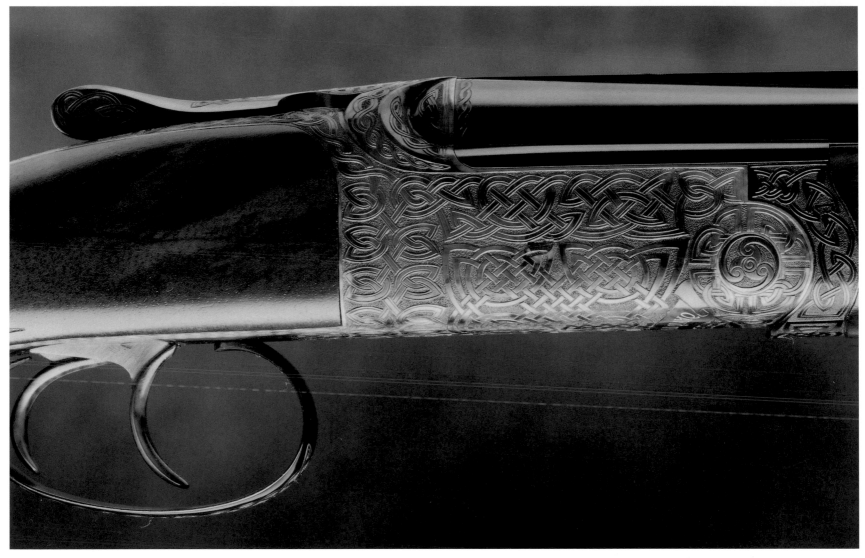

A new .410 round-action over-and-under by David McKay Brown with Celtic engraving by David V. Hudson. Strapwork this intricate cannot be scaled up or down for various frame sizes, as the proportions vary with the gauge; therefore, patterns must be designed for a specific bore. (Photo: David McKay Brown)

Opposite page: Another example of Hubert W. Paton-style engraving, this time on a double rifle by Alexander Henry of Edinburgh. Henry built a double rifle with similar engraving in 1890 for Her Majesty Queen Victoria that is in the royal gun room at Sandringham.

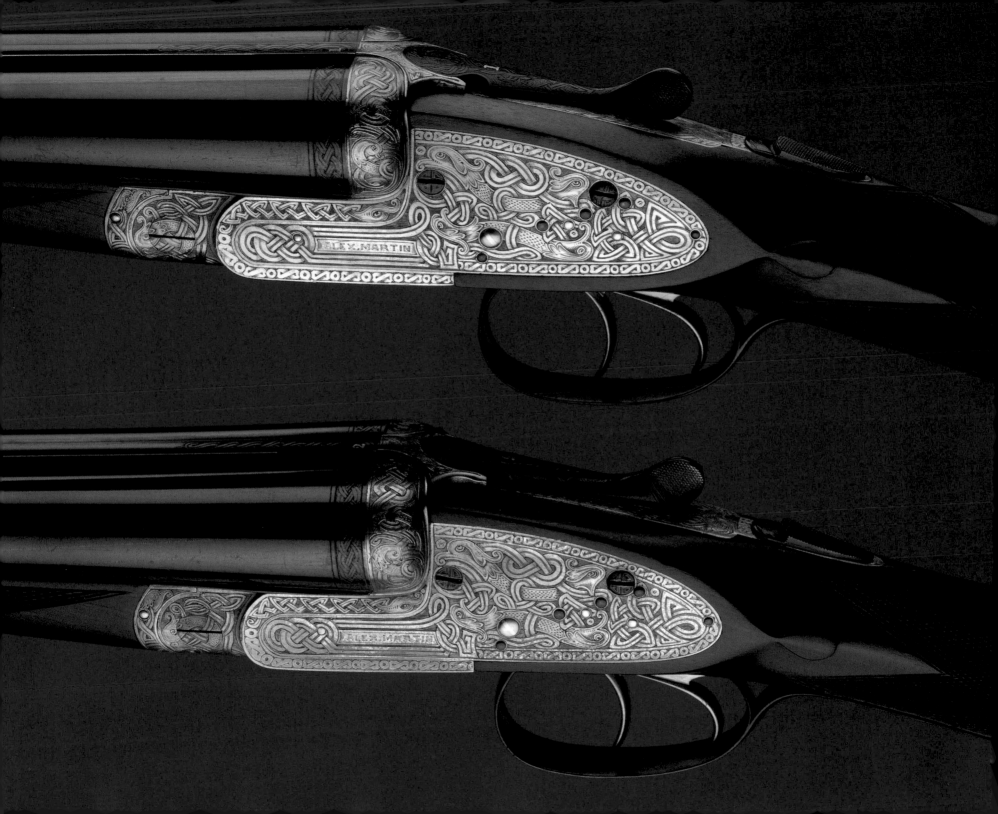

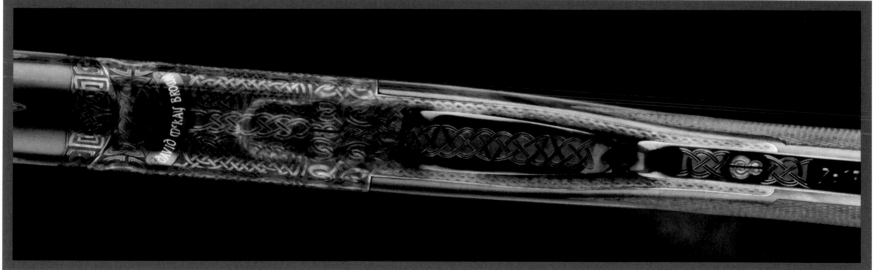

The rounded underside of the David McKay Brown .410 before and after color casehardening. The strapwork is more vivid before the final finish, while the gold-inlaid Celtic script contrasts more afterward. (Photos: David McKay Brown and David Hudson)

Opposite page: A pair of London-pattern sidelock ejectors with Celtic engraving by Alex Martin of Glasgow. Although Martin claimed that the "engraving is copied from old Celtic stone and metal ornaments,"the style of interlacing strap and knotwork with fanciful beasts is more likely taken from the title pages of illuminated manuscripts such as the Lindisfarne Gospels and the Book of Kells. Ironically, the gun was probably made and engraved in Birmingham.

Fountains of scrollwork interspersed with floral motif. The hatched, matte ground provides much of the drama. (Photo: H&H)

Chapter 5
ARTS AND CRAFTS

In the film *Red River*, John Ireland tells Montgomery Clift, "There are only two things more beautiful than a good gun—a Swiss watch or a woman from anywhere." He was wrong about the watch.

Ireland was talking about Colt revolvers and Winchester rifles, which are certainly the most perfectly proportioned American machine-made weapons. But the most beautiful gun in the world is still the British-made sidelock ejector. The sensuously shaped locks, the stocks marbled like the endplates of rare books, and barrels that taper like altar candles come together to form the most elegant of guns. The British "best" continues to set the standard by which the gunmakers of Eibar, Liege, and Val Trompia are judged.

It has always been so—at least since the midpoint of Victoria's reign, when the new, quickly reloaded breechloaders made

driven shooting possible. The crowned heads of Europe, and those of India too, flocked to Britain and bought best breechloaders in London on their way to battues at Sandringham and Balmoral.

Today, in an age of sports stars and media celebrities, it is impossible to imagine the effect that royalty had on the popular imagination. Before television, cinema, CDs, and organized team sports, the only cultural role models were royalty and their close allies, the upper ten thousand. Where they led, everyone else followed.

Packs of spectators turned out to watch Victoria's sons and other great shots of the day compete for the biggest bags. Those who could afford it emulated their betters, and the new passion for shooting provided an unprecedented windfall for the gun trade. The increased demand for guns, fortunately, occurred at a time when military

weapons were beginning to be made by machine, so there was a surplus of skilled workers to step into the breech.

But beautiful guns demand beautiful engraving, and good engravers proved difficult to find. As previously mentioned, jewelry engravers stepped in, particularly in Birmingham, where the jewelry quarter and the gun quarter lay adjacent to one another. In 1870 a decorative motif borrowed from the backs of pocket watches began to appear on the locks of sporting guns: the bouquet of roses, or rose and scroll. So quintessentially English, rose and scroll may have originated in Birmingham, but it eventually became the premier engraving style of the London gun trade.

A fashion for breechloaders, a fad for shooting, and now a fresh decorative style—over the next few decades every gunmaker in London jumped on the bandwagon by offering some variation of

This Holland & Holland engraved with a bold leaf pattern was clearly inspired by Arts and Crafts design. (Photo: Holland & Holland)

The tendrils of open foliate scroll here appear to be suspended from a trellis of Celtic-inspired strapwork. (Photo: H&H)

Stylized dog roses emerge from a cornucopia in this unique take on bouquet and scroll. (Photo: H&H)

bouquet and scroll engraving. Or almost everyone; Holland & Holland, a firm with a reputation for colorfully decorated presentation guns, found its inspiration in an entirely different direction—the Arts and Crafts movement and the fertile mind of William Morris.

William Morris was born in Walthamstow in 1834, and he enjoyed a privileged childhood before attending Marlborough College and Exeter College, Oxford. The first son of an affluent businessman, Morris was groomed for a career in the church. Inspired by the social criticism of John Ruskin and fascinated by medieval art and decoration, he became articled to G. E. Street, the leading neo-Gothic architect of the day. But he soon left, having fallen under the influence of Dante Gabriel Rossetti and the Pre-Raphaelites.

By the 1860s it was clear that Morris's creative future lay with the decorative arts. His success as a designer was ensured when he decorated the Red House, Bexleyheath, which led to the founding of a company that subsequently became "Morris & Co." The firm was well known for its stained glass windows, which are often characterized by scrolling foliage patterns. In 1890 Morris founded the Kelmscott Press and adapted scrolling foliage, such as the fruiting vine, as decorative borders for the pages of the books he published. His greatest achievements as a designer were the contiguous patterns he produced for textiles and wallpaper. The best of these, such as "Acanthus" from 1875, were masterpieces of stylized nature.

To some extent, Morris and his designs were a reaction to the horrors of the Industrial Revolution. His call for the revival of the medieval tradition of craftsmanship was one of the main influences behind the foundation of the Arts and Crafts movement. Like his friends the Pre-Raphaelites, he found his inspiration in an earlier age, when arts and crafts held sway over machinery. Classic, Gothic, and above all me-

William Morris's design of acanthus wallpaper. (Photo: William Morris Gallery, London Borough of Waltham Forest)

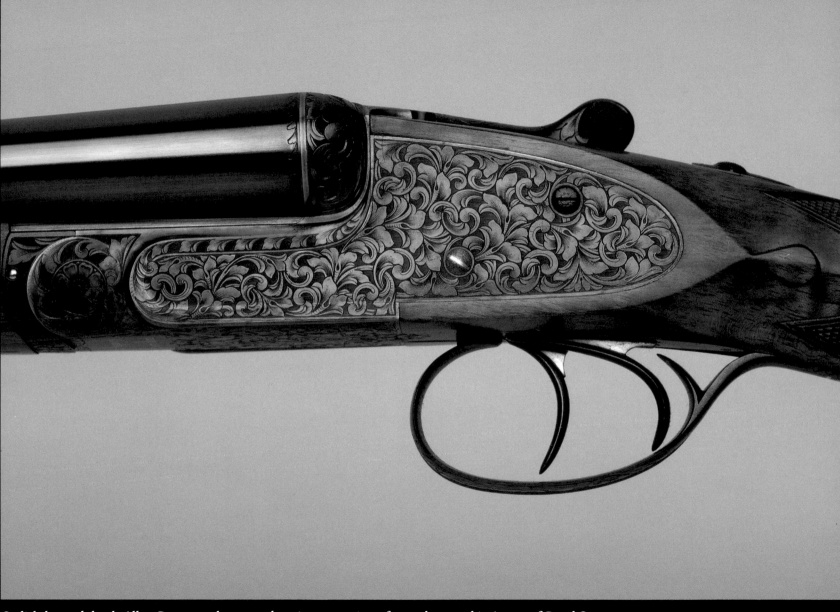

Stylish but subdued, Allan Portsmouth postmodern interpretation of acanthus on this Asprey of Bond Street.

A W. R. Pape of Newcastle with Arts and Crafts engraving. The maker's ledgers record the style as "floral cut" and the engraver as "Woodruffe."

Above: Fruiting vine by Woodruffe

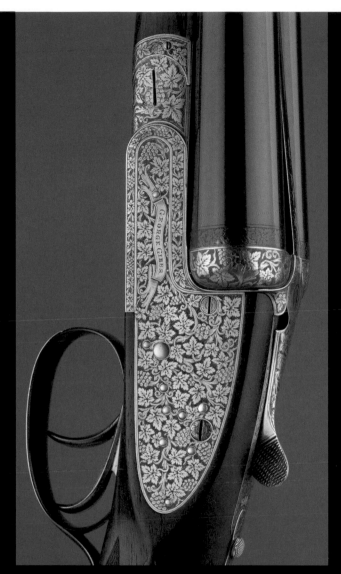

Above: Fruiting vine by Harry Morris

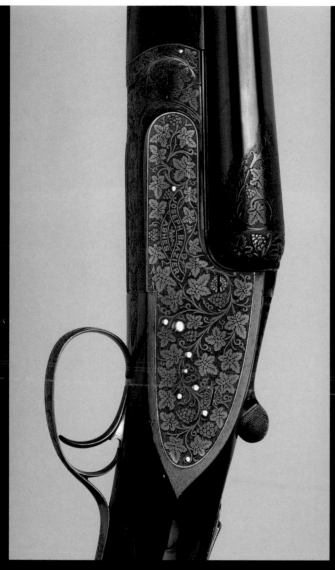

Above: Fruiting vine by Kell

dieval influences dominate his work. Morris was particularly enamored of these earlier traditions when they inscribed the forms of nature on the handiwork of man, such as the use of acanthus leaves on Corinthian capitals. Paradoxically, however, his designs were new. He took old images, such as the acanthus designs on Greek columns, and stylized them to the point where they must have seemed the essence of modernity to design-conscious Victorians: Some of the later designs even have a nascent Art Nouveau look to them.

One legacy of the Arts and Crafts movement was the effect it had on gun engraving. The fruiting vine design that was featured in the Kelmscott Press books was widely copied and can frequently be found on old guns by Coster of Glasgow, Gibbs of Bristol, and Pape of Newcastle-upon-Tyne, as well as on new ones by William Evans of St. James. As recently as the 1950s an engraver, coincidentally named Morris, this time Harry Morris, made a specialty of the design; during a visit to Birmingham, I was shown his original template for fruiting vine.

Numerous gunmakers borrowed, eclectically, from the William Morris portfolio, but only one accepted his manifesto wholeheartedly, and only one applied the inspiration of the Arts and Crafts movement to all of their guns. A tobacconist from Holborn named Harris Holland founded Holland & Holland in 1835; the firm became H&H when Harris made his nephew a partner in 1876. Holland & Holland grew throughout the 1860s and 1870s with the increasing popularity of shooting. They must have been searching for some way to make their product distinctive from those of their major rivals: Boss, Purdey, and Woodward, all of whom used bouquet and scroll as a decorative motif.

Harry Morris in his Birmingham workshop. (Photo: Geoffrey Boothroyd)

By the time of Harris Holland's death in 1896, Henry Holland had discovered the Arts and Crafts movement, and with it the decorative style the firm needed to set itself apart from its peers. Few Holland guns with bouquet and scroll survive, suggesting that the pattern was rarely used. Instead, every kind of Arts and Crafts device, motif, and design was explored, exploited, and extrapolated, until the style became Holland & Holland's own.

Acanthus, in particular, with all its classical allusions, became the ornament of choice. The Victorians, who thought of themselves and their culture as descending directly from Greek and Roman civilization, would have known that Helen had worn a veil fringed with acanthus when she arrived in Troy and that the Corinthians used the same leaves to decorate the capitals of their columns. In 1875 William Morris produced an acanthus wallpaper design that was, to that time, by far his most ambitious. It was later adapted to a scale suitable for gunlocks, where it became a signature feature of Holland & Holland guns.

This was not the first time that acanthus had appeared as a motif for weapons. In Renaissance Italy, Benvenuto Cellini had written about its use on daggers:

> Turkish foliage work is based on arum leaves, with a few small sunflowers, and, although this is quite pretty, unlike our designs it soon loses its charm. In Italy we have several kinds of foliage design. The Lombards do very beautiful work by copying the leaves of bryony and ivy, in magnificent loops that are very pleasing to the eye. The Tuscans and Romans improve greatly on this because they copy the leaves of the acanthus, commonly known as bears foot, and show its stems and flowers all twisting and turning. It gives a charming effect if one has some birds and various kinds of animals engraved on the work as well, and his choice here shows what sort of taste the artist has.

Cellini's engraving style would have been pure anathema to William Morris, with his highly developed Pre-Raphaelite sensibilities. He and the entire Arts and Crafts movement found their inspiration in an earlier era.

Throughout Edwardian times Holland & Holland used William Morris-inspired engraving patterns to distinguish themselves from their rivals. Their fin de siècle double rifles frequently featured Arts and Crafts designs with Celtic overtones. Recently, when H&H needed a unique engraving style to help launch a new range of over-and-under shotguns, the engraving team brought some of these designs up to date with results that were appropriate, tasteful, and respectful of Holland's Arts and Crafts legacy.

Today there is no reason why Holland & Holland's affinity for Arts and Crafts designs should not continue. As long as there are clients who are searching for an engraving style less conservative than traditional bouquet and scroll yet more deeply incised than bulino, Holland & Holland's Arts and Crafts-inspired style will always find devotees.

A 10-bore Paradox ball and shotgun built for the Raja of Mudhol by Holland & Holland and finished in 1905. The engraving of strapwork pierced with burgeoning acanthus is typical of Holland guns from the turn of the century. This style would provide the inspiration for decorating the current generation of Holland & Holland over-and-under game and sporting-clay guns; in its modern incarnation it has become known as "banner scroll." The name Paradox was adopted in 1885 when Holland & Holland introduced the system of rifling invented by Colonel George Vincent Fosbery of the Bengal Army, which had shallow rifling in the choke extending back a couple of inches from the muzzle. The conical bullet traveled up the smooth bore until it struck the rifling and got a last-instant stabilizing spin for nose-on flight. The gun could also be used as a shotgun, and one testimonial claimed, "I have killed everything with it from tiger to snipe."

Chapter 6

THE PRINCELY LEGACY

British gun engraving is typically thought of as conservative, restrained, even severe. This is unfortunate, since English artisans have traditionally enjoyed a long love affair with the East, an area where a more opulent aesthetic is celebrated. One authority, Dr. Frederic A. Harris, in his book *Firearms Engraving as Decorative Art,* even attributes the origins of English scrollwork to the palm frond, "which clearly has the corresponding form and occurs frequently as an Islamic decorative element." Dr. Harris may be right, although at this late date it is impossible to know for certain. What is certain, however, is that the influence of oriental fashions on mainstream decorative art trickled down to gun embellishers.

During the eighteenth century when cabinetmakers such as Thomas Chippendale and goldsmiths such as William Cripps were influenced by chinoiserie-style ornamentation, London gunmakers employed silversmiths to inlay their gunstocks with fantastic compositions of rococo scrollwork enclosing Chinese figures. William Bailes was one such gunmaker, and in his efforts to master chinoiserie-style ornamentation he employed Jeconiah Ashley to do his silver work. A little later, when John Nash was rebuilding Brighton Pavilion in the pseudo-oriental style, H. W. Mortimer, gunmaker to King George III, built several pistols decorated in the "Turkish taste." But no one could have accused British gunmakers of creating really opulent guns until the maharajas came along.

Maharaja is a Sanskrit word meaning "great king." It was applied to all Indian princes, their importance being measured by the number of salvos fired in the gun salute that greeted their appearance. For instance, among the maharajas whose guns are illustrated here, the Nizam of Hyderabad warranted the maximum twenty-one-gun-salute; Karauli merited an impressive seventeen guns; Mudhol only nine; while Piagur was the ruler of a small "non salute" state.

The Indian princes emerged at the beginning of the nineteenth century but did not enjoy real security of tenure until after the Mutiny (or the First War of Independence, if you are Indian) in 1858. This security evaporated after another armed conflict, when India eventually won her independence in the wake of World War II. In the short ninety years of their ascendancy the ma-

Rigby sidelock rifle, serial number 18,191, was made in October 1932 for the Maharaja of Karauli and was the last double rifle built with a vertical-rising bolt (Rigby & Bissell patent 1141 of 1879). It is engraved by Harry Kell with gold-inlaid crest on the lockplates, with an original caliber of .350 (No. 2) rebored, circa 1980, to 9.3x74R.

harajas enjoyed unprecedented wealth. Never in the field of human conduct was so much levied on so many by so few, as Churchill might have said.

Great wealth with few responsibilities engendered a playboy lifestyle, and the princes lavished money on monumental palaces, luxury cars, and extravagant ceremonies. As Rudyard Kipling put it: "Providence created the Maharajas to offer mankind a spectacle." They were also all, or almost all, sportsmen. Many were handicapped polo players, several captained national cricket sides, but mostly they were sportsmen in the nineteenth-century sense of the word, which is to say they relished field sports.

In the west, the Maharaja of Bhavnagar maintained the ancient tradition of coursing black buck with cheetahs. Over the course of a lifetime he imported a total thirty-two of these, the fastest of cats, from British East Africa, after indigenous populations dwindled to nothing. Another cat, the lynxlike caracal, was employed in the same state to pursue the Indian antelope known as the chinkara.

In the dry country of the northwest, the Maharaja of Bikaner enjoyed sand grouse shooting on the grand scale. When the Prince of Wales arrived in 1905, 100,000 birds came to drink at the Gajner Lake, and a good morning's bag was 4,000 birds. Seventeen years later Yvonne Fitzroy in her book *Courts and Camps in India* documented another big day:

> It is an extraordinary sight even when watched, as I watched from a respectful distance, and sounds more like a brisk engagement at the front than a morning's

H. H. THE MAHARAJAH OF KARAULI

The Maharaja of Karauli.

pastime. The grouse are kept away from the other tanks in the countryside for several days before the shoot, with the result that they all sweep down on Gajner for their morning drink. Not in hundreds but in thousands, not for half an hour but for three full hours on end. From every direction they come, flying at a tremendous rate in perfect military formation—scouts, vanguard, main body, reinforcements, all complete. They make very difficult shooting and in the best butts the business is incessant; the Princes usually use three guns apiece and have two loaders each. On one occasion eight hundred birds fell to the Maharaja Kumar alone, to a total of sixteen hundred cartridges—a magnificent average.

A Charles Lancaster double rifle in .280 with quarry species of the subcontinent inlaid in the naive style on the leg o'mutton locks and action body. Even the instructions for clamping the main spring are in gold. The rifle was one of a pair built for H. H. Col. Nawab Mohamed Afaidalla Khan, circa 1912.

The griffins, serpents, and mythical beasts on this .577, Modele de Luxe, double rifle built for the Raja of Mudhol in 1913 are usually engraved only on Holland & Holland double rifles. In 1986 an article appeared claiming that "only one workman at Holland's ever did this type of engraving." In fact, many engravers produced their own interpretation of this style, including Harry Corbett and Ken Preater.

This huge .600 double rifle built for Raja Bindesh Wari Prasad Singh of Piagpur by R. B. Rodda & Co. of 2 Wellesley Place, Calcutta, was probably built in the Birmingham gun-quarter. The Indian game scene is cleverly integrated into a textured background of palm fronds and stippling.

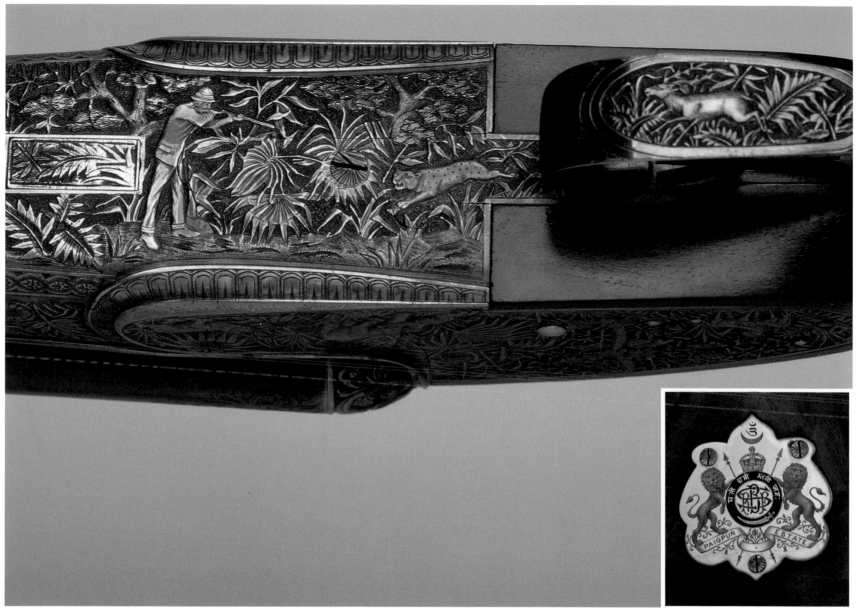

The underside of the Piagpur Rodda features a realistic representation of, perhaps, Raja Singh in a tropical linen suit and pith helmet bracing himself before a charging leopard, an animal more usually referred to as a panther in India.

Raja Singh of Piagpur's family crest appears on the stock.

A Holland & Holland Model Deluxe .375 Magnum flanged double rifle built for the Nizam of Hyderabad. It features the Nizam's crest, has serial number 32181 and according to Holland & Holland was probably engraved by Harry Kell. (Photo: Raj and Jeet Singh)

The Sixth Nizam of Hyderabad.

This gold-inlaid Purdey hammer rifle with grip safety and isolated locks was presented to the Honourable Sir Digbijoy, Sing Bahadoor, the Maharajah of Balrampore, in March 1870, by H. R. H. the Duke of Edinburgh. (Photo: Raj and Jeet Singh)

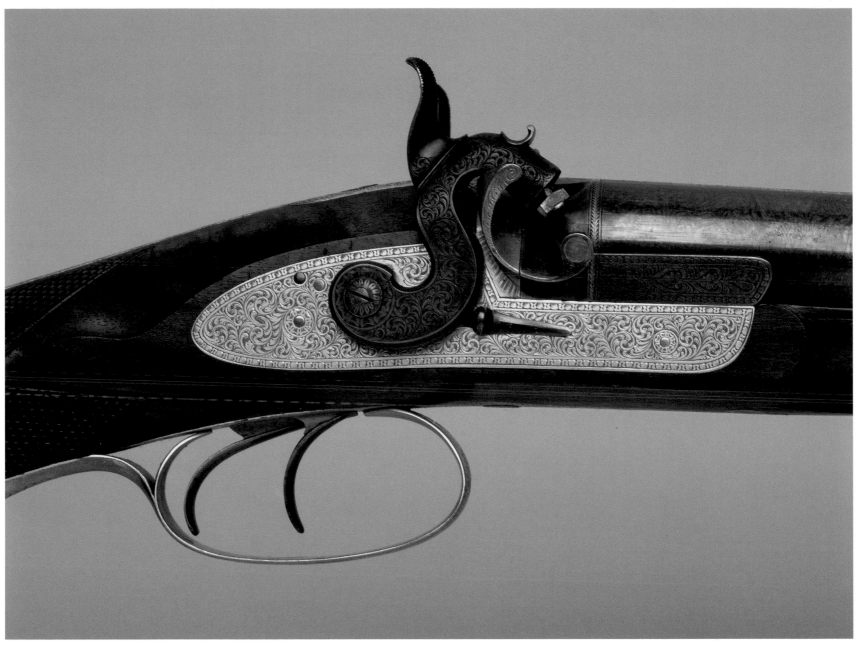

A presentation muzzleloader by Bond & James of Birmingham with gold Damascened lockwork. The gun is obviously of high quality. Ironically, the Bond & James name is more often associated with the Africa trade, where guns of low quality were exchanged for slaves, than with maharajas.

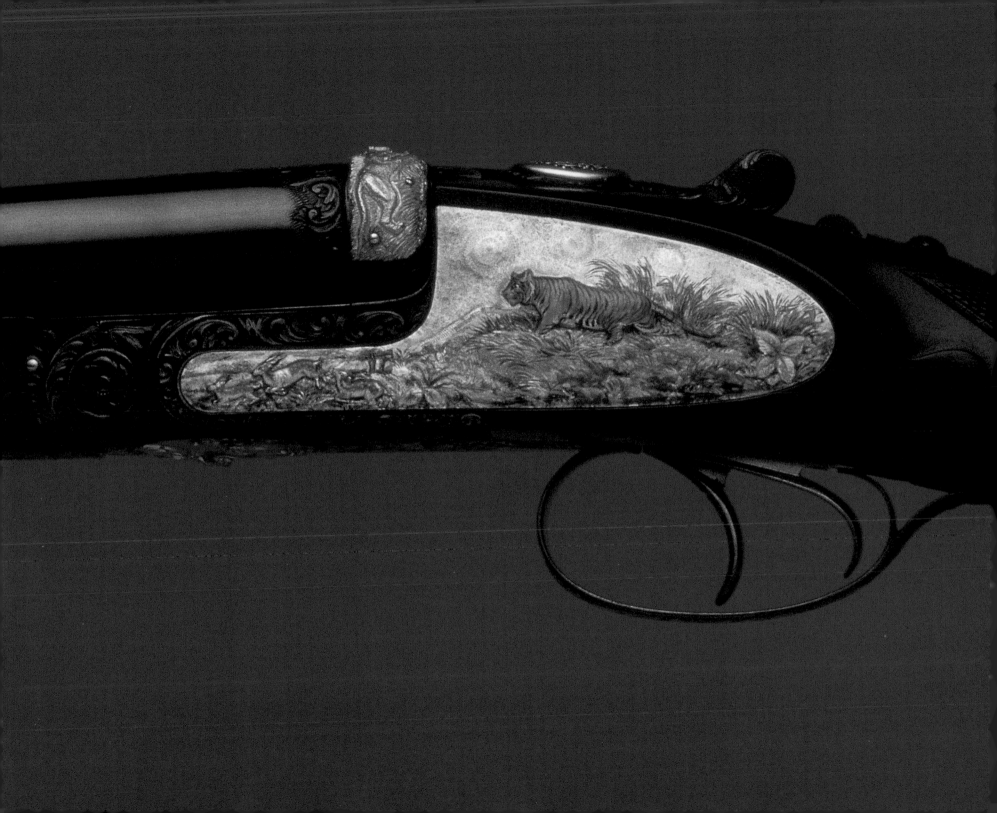

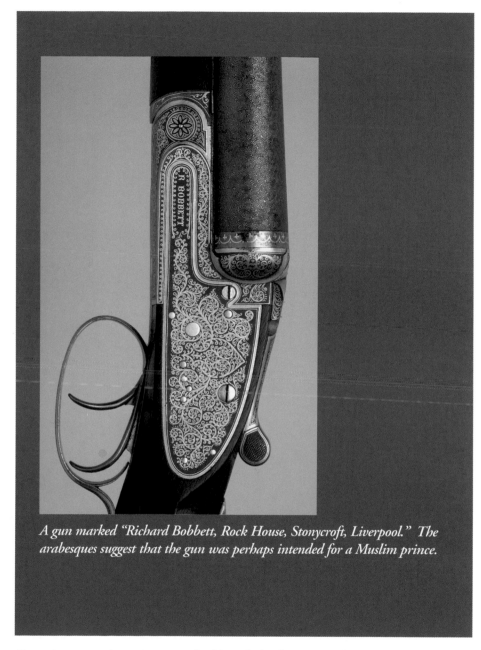

A gun marked "Richard Bobbett, Rock House, Stonycroft, Liverpool." The arabesques suggest that the gun was perhaps intended for a Muslim prince.

In the middle of the country not far from Delhi and Agra another lake, known as the Ghana Jheel, provided the best duck shooting in the Empire. With fifty permanent blinds dotted around its ten-mile-square expanse, the lake was shot only three times a year to ensure big bags.

In the east of the country, a small state in Bengal—situated about halfway between Bhutan and the southward bend of the Brahmaputra—boasted big-game shooting that rivaled that of Africa. Over the course of a lifetime the Maharaja of Cooch Behar shot a total of 438 buffalo and 311 leopard, but in this ultimate competition of Indian princely life it was the tigers that really mattered: Cooch Behar shot 365, while the Maharaja of Rewa shot 481. In the thirteenth edition of Rowland Ward's record book it was claimed that the Maharaja of Sirguja killed a total of 1,600!

The lavishness of the lifestyle was exceeded only by the opulence of the hardware required to pursue it: Bhavnagar needed an open tourer to transport his cheetahs, and Patuala bought a hydroplane to keep his ducks from alighting on his *jheel*. Everyone who was anyone had to have his collection of ornate double rifles and shotguns. In Calcutta, which was the capital of British India before 1912, Walter Locke & Co., Manton & Co., R. B. Rodda, and Lyon & Lyon offered guns and rifles in every imaginable caliber, from tiny .410 collector's guns to massive .600 double rifles suitable for India's biggest game.

Opposite page: A .375 express double rifle built in 1912 for Colonel Obaidulla Khan by Holland & Holland. The maker's records reveal more about contemporary Indian taste than the photo: ".375 Modele de Luxe, hammerless ejector cordite rifle, treble grip, 28" barrels, special lockplates in gold and enamel. Gold leopard in relief on each fence. Monogram on top lever in gold plate with diamonds, rubies, emeralds." Like many H&H doubles of this era intended for the subcontinent, this rifle is fitted with false lockplates that are enameled in high relief. Some were even said to have been enameled in a Wedgwood pattern with figures in white cameo relief on a matte blue background. (Photo: Butterfield & Butterfield)

An Alex Henry muzzle loader built for an Indian prince. (Photo: Raj and Jeet Singh)

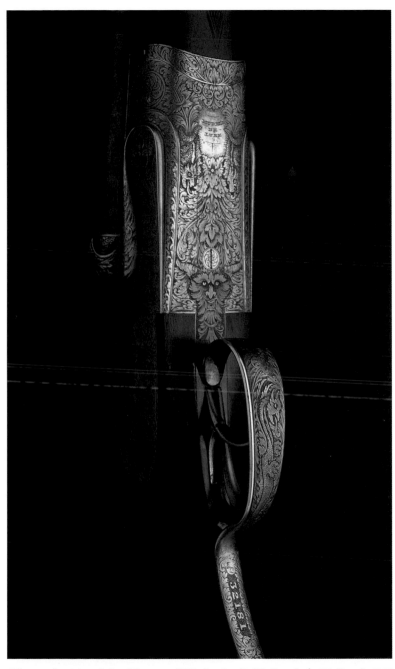

The underside of the Nizam of Hyderabad's Holland & Holland .375 flanged magnum double rifle.(Photo: Raj and Jeet Singh)

The "nonsalute" minor princes went to the middlemen in Calcutta, but those who could afford to do so bought their guns and rifles in London. Holland & Holland was a particular favorite; Cooch Behar considered them "second to none" for rifles. The truly rich maharajas had their guns and rifles inlaid with gold, or they had enameled dummy lockplates fitted. Some even had foresights of precious stones.

The benefit to the British gun trade was enormous, but not everyone approved of such ostentatious taste. Writing about weapons made in the East, Sir Guy Laking, Hon. Inspector of the Armouries, circa 1913, pointed out that "there is always the prejudice against the weapon of the Orient, that costliness of material is ever uppermost over the fertility of design and fineness of the workmanship." Fair enough when Indian workmanship was involved, but this did not hold true with London guns built for the maharajas and decorated in the Indian style.

Not that there ever was a single "Indian style": The Nizam of Hyderabad, a Sunni Muslim, avoided the depiction of living creatures on his weapons—although they were not strictly proscribed by the Koran—reasoning that to do so was an infringement of the sole power of God to create life. The Maharaja of Alwar was a strict Hindu who owned no article of cowhide, so his guns were supplied with rubber pads and cheek pieces, and the cases were made of oak with canvas covers. Across the subcontinent, cultural diversity was at least as great as, and perhaps a lot greater than, it was in

Details of Purdey rifle presented by the Duke of Edinburgh to the Maharajah of Balrampore.(Photo: Raj and Jeet Singh)

all of Europe. This diversity was expressed in the objets d'art—including weapons—ordered by the princes.

The maharajas did not disappear with Indian independence, although a new democratic government curbed their lifestyle dramatically. Many of the guns they owned are now in American collections. Their legacy, at least as far as decorated weapons are concerned, is that incomparable wealth and flamboyant embellishment combined to bring out the best in London and Birmingham gunmakers. Those guns are some of the finest ever produced by the British gun trade.

PART TWO

Chapter 7

THE PLATES

Opposite page: A Nelson-built Boss-style over-and-under with bas-relief game scene and gold-inlay vignettes against a foliate scroll background by Alan Brown. Just in front of the bar, golden quail escape into the distance through a thicket of scrolling acanthus.

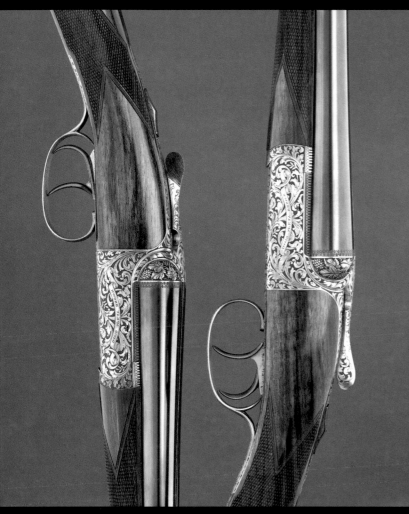 

The Brown Brothers are responsible for the engraving on this pair of round action guns by David McKay Brown.

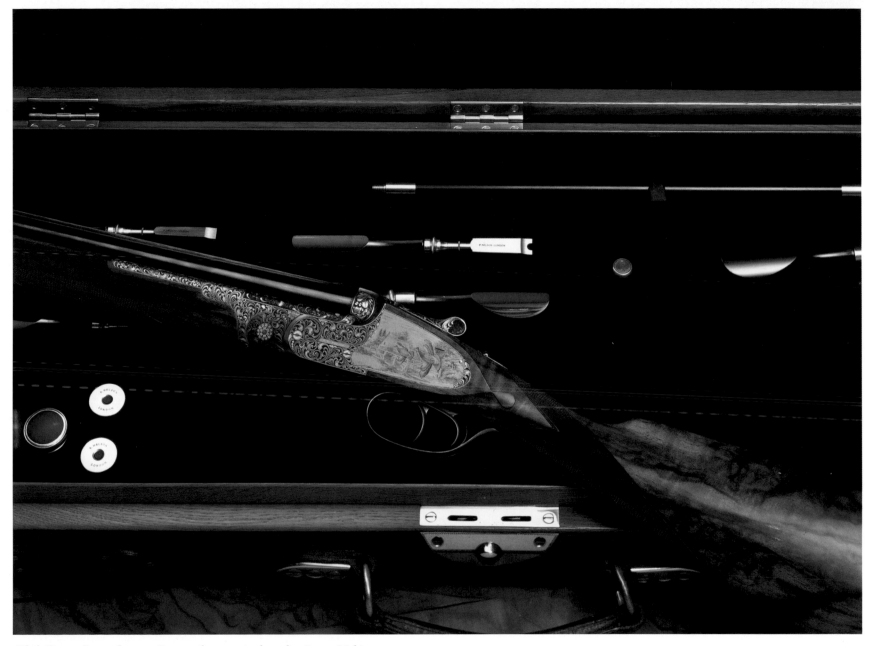

Phil Coggan's work on a Boss style over and under Peter Nelson.

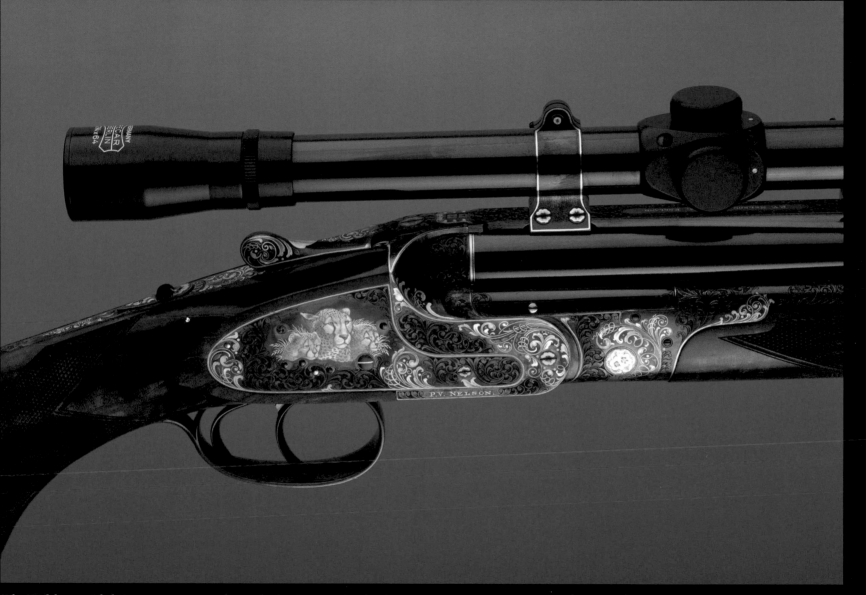

The Welshman Phil Coggan is getting the credit he deserves for developing the multicolored flush-gold inlay style of engraving on this Boss-style over-and-under .375 flanged double rifle by P. V. Nelson.

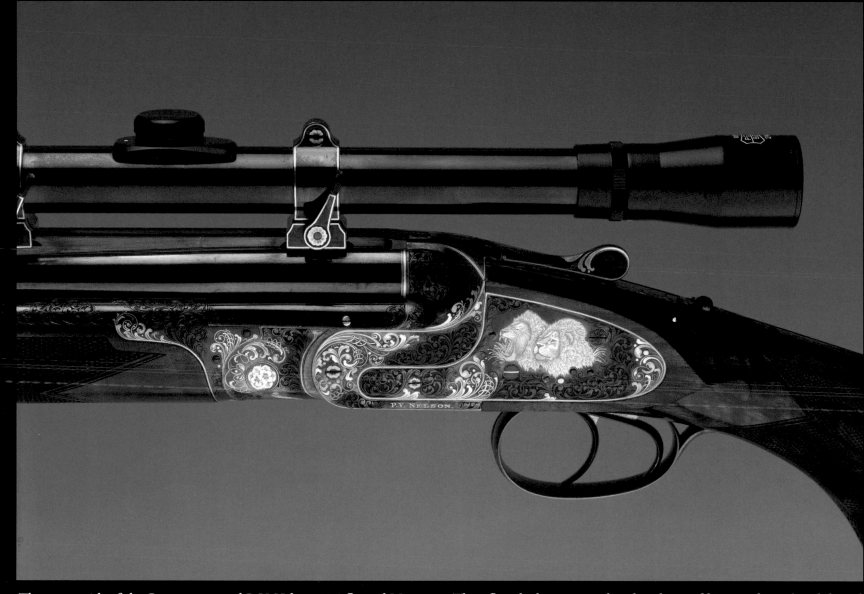

The reverse side of the Coggan-engraved P. V. Nelson .375 flanged Magnum. The rifle, which is engraved with a theme of big cats, has 24-inch barrels and weighs 10 lbs.

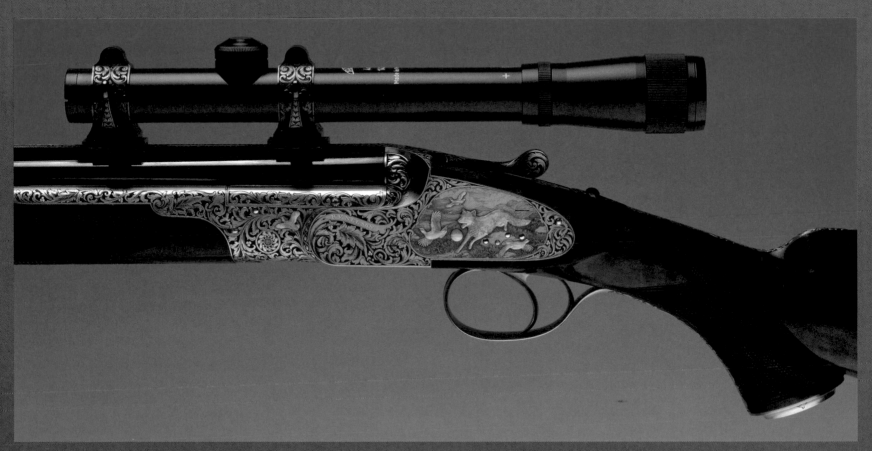

A Brown-engraved Peter Nelson in .218 Bee with single trigger, which also has interchangeable .410 barrels. The gun weighs 6 lbs., 12 oz. with the 24-inch rifle barrels, and 5 lbs., 10 oz. with the 28-inch shotgun barrels.

On the underside, red-legged partridge flush across a plowed field, and a woodcock is centered on the trigger guard. The serial number on the tang corresponds to the caliber.

The underside of the Coggan-engraved P. V. Nelson showing a leopard ready to pounce.

Multicolored gold is used on the butt cap to create a bouquet of wild roses.

Opposite page: The Big Five theme on the left lockplate with Cape buffalo surprised by a hooded cobra, while the king of beasts looks on from the detonators.

A heavy Purdey double rifle with bas-relief carving by the Brown brothers. The caliber is .600, suitable for Africa's largest game. Appropriately, the rifle is engraved with a theme of the Big Five, with rhino on the lockplates and leopard on the side-clipped detonators.

A lion is represented on the butt cap of the .600 Purdey.

An elephant with skin real enough to put egrets to flight.

(closeup) A private joke between patron and craftsman appears in great detail at the foot of the elephant. A boom rat—so well executed that its eye is visible—represents the client who was born in the year of the rat and the engraver, whose nickname is "boomer."

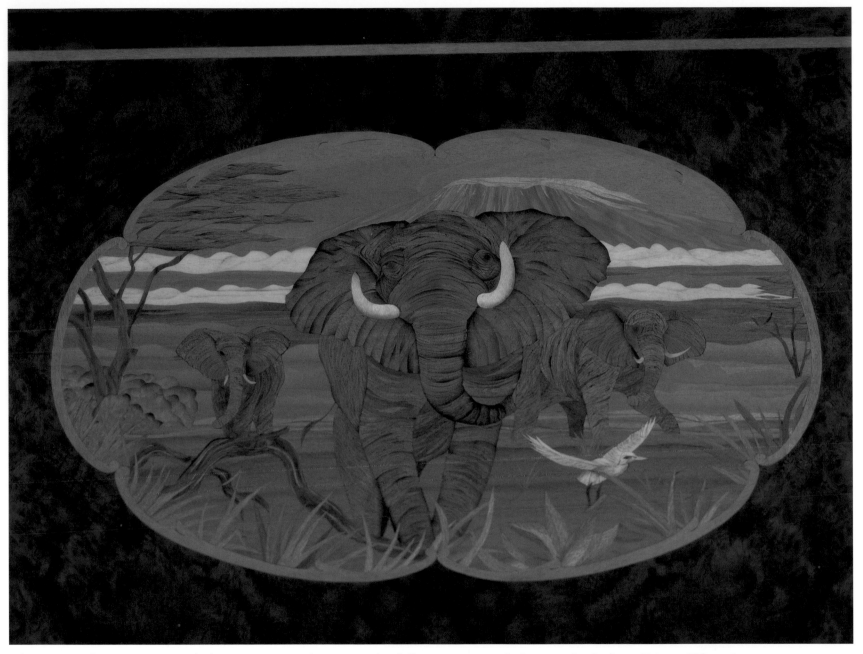

The Big Five theme continues with the marquetry case by Vince Rickard illustrating angry elephants in the shadow of Mount Kilimanjaro.

The Purdey .600 with every imaginable accoutrement, cased by Vince Rickard.

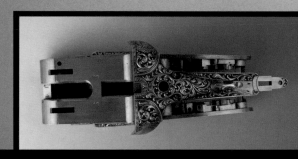

A lion roars from the detonators as a pair of bulls battle it out in Amboseli National Park on this Purdey with Phil Coggan engraving.

The top view of the Coggan-engraved Purdey with bolted safety.

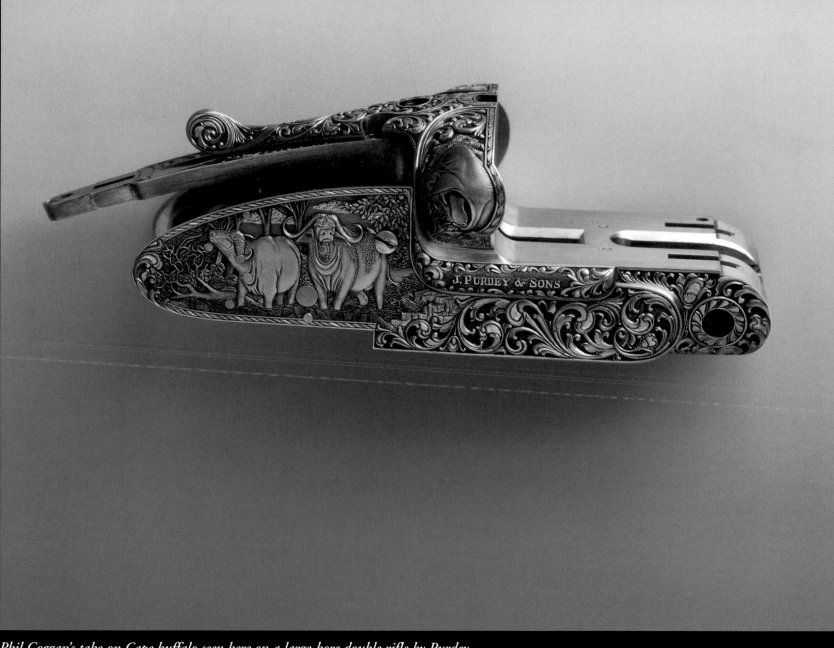

Phil Coggan's take on Cape buffalo seen here on a large-bore double rifle by Purdey.

This .470 double rifle by Peter V. Nelson has a fluted bolster and skirmishing rhinos by the Brown brothers.

The Browns have mixed a variety of techniques from bulino on the lockplates to deep carving on the bolster and detonators to create drama on this .470 double rifle by Peter V. Nelson.

The background detail here is impressive, with an African weaver returning to a nesting colony in a thorn tree.

Opposite page: A trio of round-bodied Boss-style guns by Peter V. Nelson with vignettes by the Brown brothers representing English game shooting in 1800, 1850, and 1900.

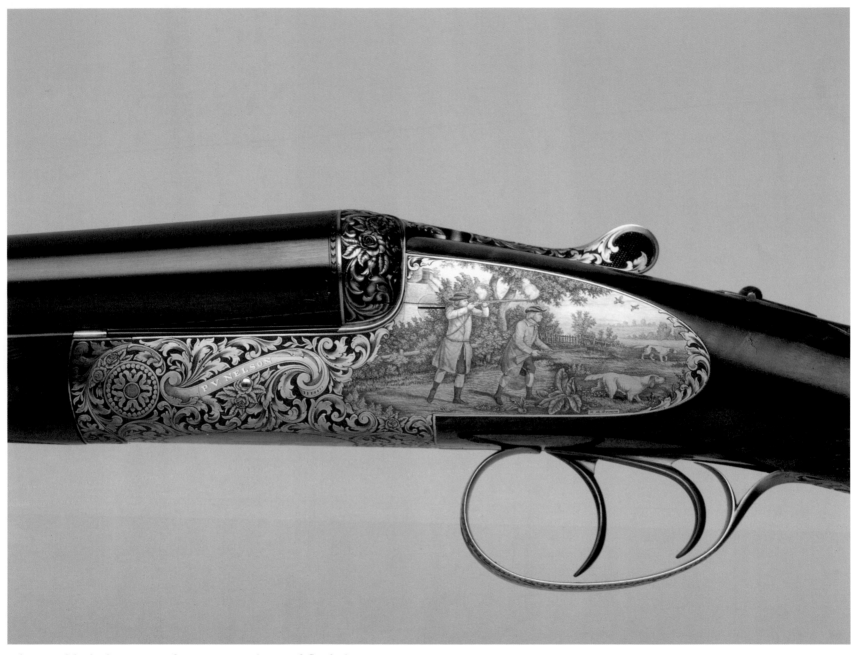

The round-bodied 1800 gun features tricorn hats and flintlocks.

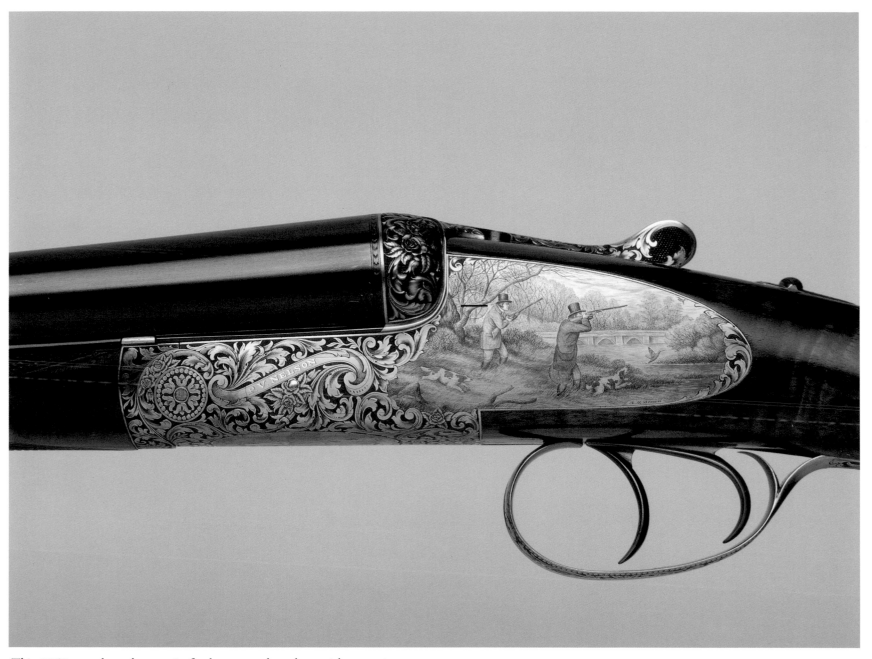

This 1850 gun shows hunters in frock coats and top hats with percussion guns.

In 1987 the Brown brothers completed a commission for Holland & Holland of rococo-style relief engraving on a .410 with beavertail fore-end. A decade later they reprised the theme on this 28-bore by Purdey. Clearly they have not been standing still these last ten years.

Opposite page: Scene depicting the end of a successful day in 1850.

The left lockplate shows Mars being adored by Venus.

Cephalus and Aurora—Cephalus (son of Hermes) was married to Procris but was unwittingly seduced by Aurora. Artemis (Diana), angered by Cephalus' adultery, caused him to accidentally shoot his beloved Procris whilst out hunting.

The case disk features Eos or Aurora (dawn) risen at the close of night, ascending to heaven to announce the coming of the morning light.

The grip cap shows the head of Medusa—one of the three Gorgons, the sight of whose head would turn the beholder to stone. Perseus beheaded Medusa.

The heelplate features Cupid and Psyche. Aphrodite, jealous of Psyche's beauty, sent her son Cupid to cast a damning spell on Psyche. Cupid accidentally dropped one of his arrows on his own foot, however, and ended up falling in love with Psyche himself.

The gunmaker's craft is also represented in the lines and stock of the 28-bore rococo Purdey.

The sculpting has been continued onto the breech ends of the barrels.

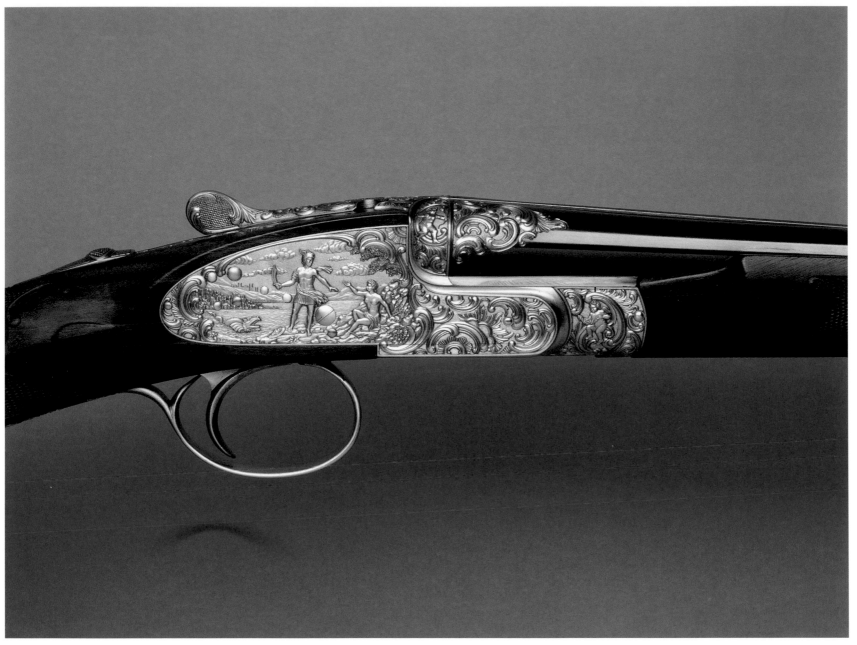

Scenes from the original fourten rococo gun built in 1987 by Holland & Holland and engraved with Perseus about to kill the sea monster before freeing Andromeda. His shield, which is at his feet, is embellished with the carved head of Medusa. (Photo: Butterfield & Butterfield)

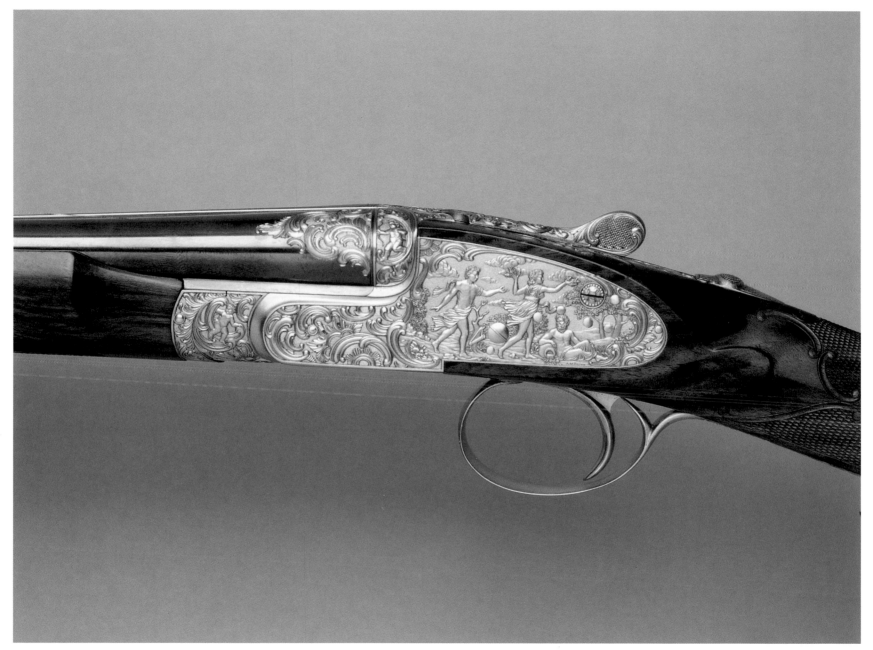

The scene from the left lockplate of the fourten rococo gun shows Apollo chasing Daphne, with the river god Peneius (her father) who turns Daphne into a laurel tree. The tableau is framed in rococo-style relief engraving. (Photo: Butterfield & Butterfield)

Aphrodite with putti on the bottom of the fourten rococo gun. (Photo: Butterfield & Butterfield)

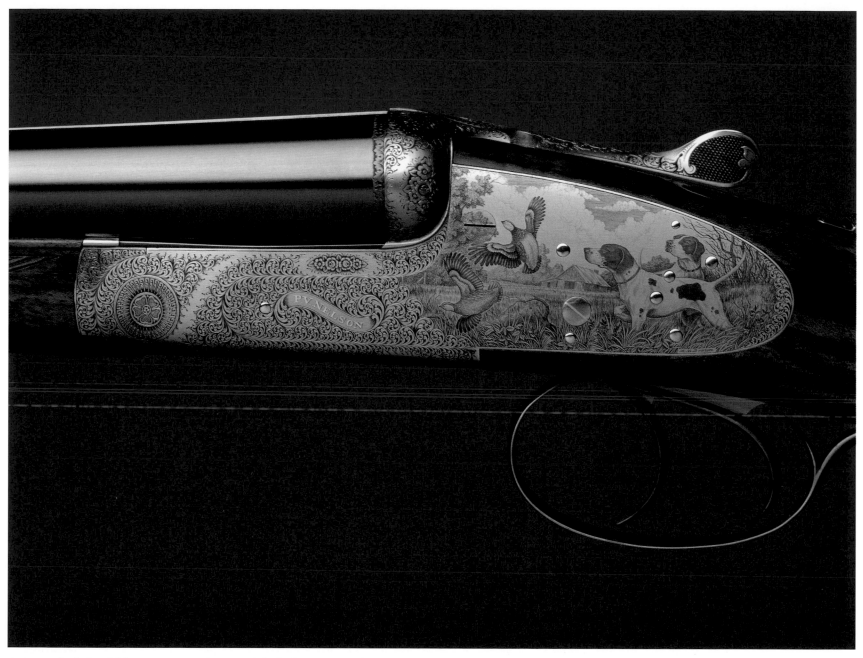

Pointers find the old barn covey on this round-bodied Peter V. Nelson gun with Brown brothers engraving.

Ken Hunt has inlaid the detonators with oak leaves and the lockplates with bobwhite quail on this Purdey game gun.

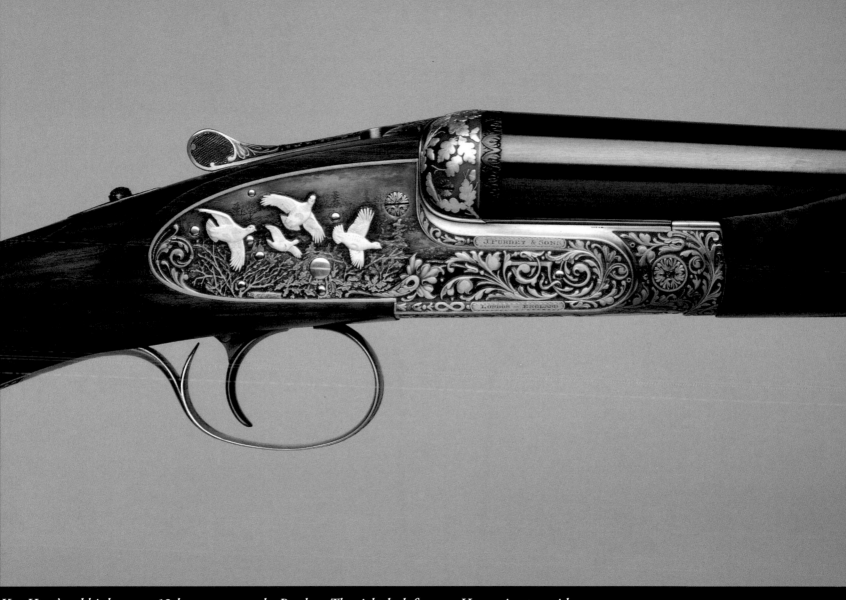

Ken Hunt's gold inlay on a 12-bore game gun by Purdey. The right lock features Hungarian partridge.

Phil Coggan's work on a Peter V. Nelson game gun.

The left side of Peter V. Nelson's gun number 1,200 with fine game-scene engraving by Phil Coggan, inspired by a David Maass painting.

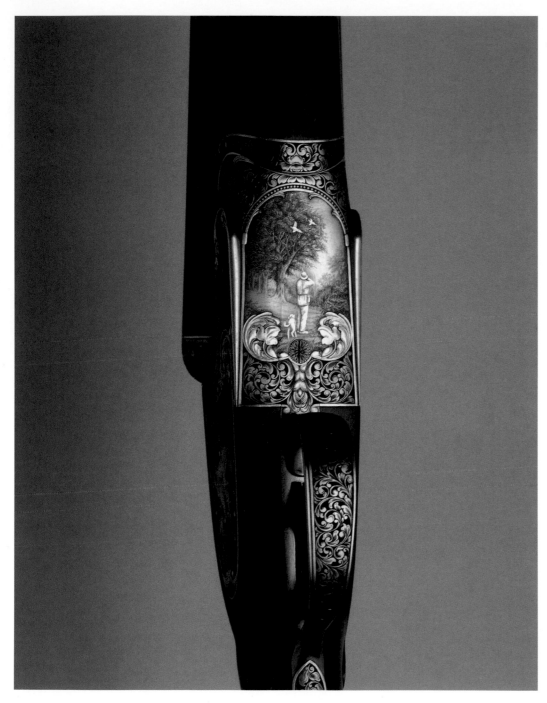

*Taking a high one on the underside of the Coggan-engraved
Peter V. Nelson gun, serial number 1,169.*

A vignette of English partridge in deep relief against a background of flat foliate scroll. The gun is an over-and-under round action by David McKay Brown, with engraving by the Brown brothers.

Alan Brown engraved these French partridge on this Beesley-actioned gun by Hartmann & Weiss.

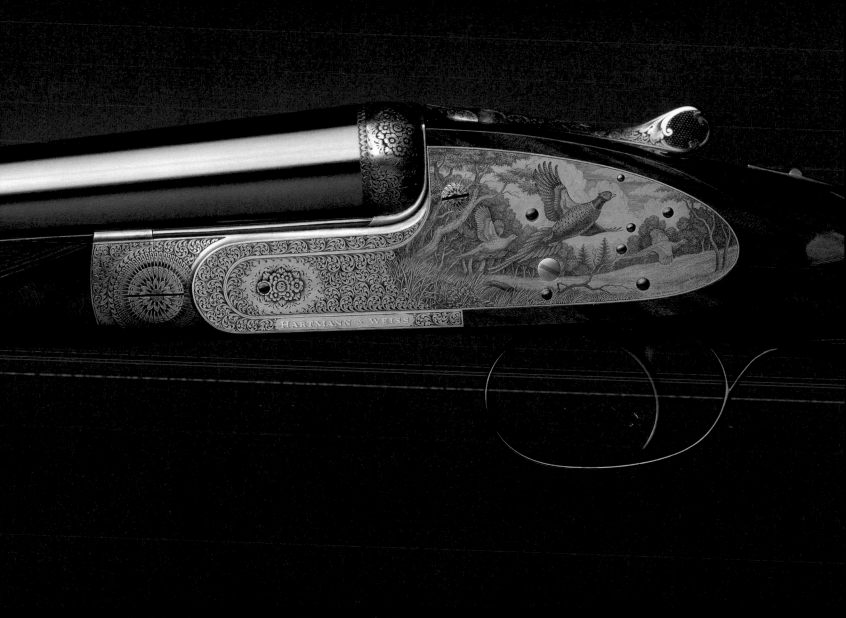

Pheasant on the left side of the Alan Brown-engraved Hartmann & Weiss.

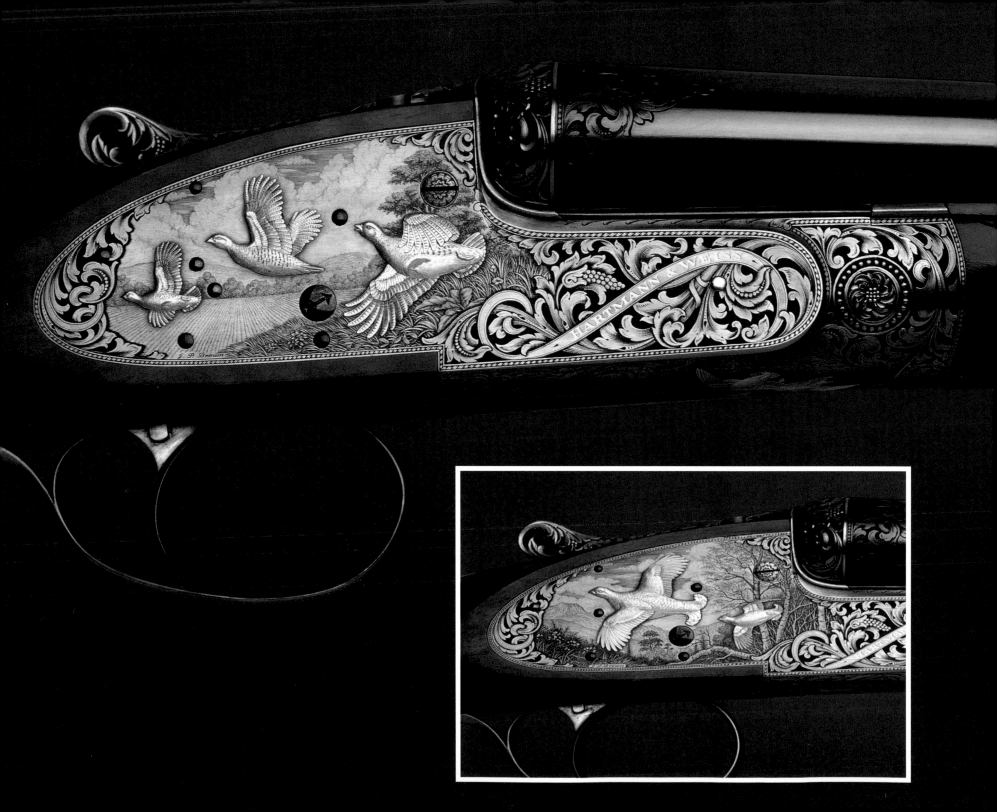

The bottoms of this 20-bore pair show woodcock and snipe in appropriate settings.

Opposite page: English partridge in a lowland setting on this 20-bore by Hartman and Weiss.
Opposite page inset: Black grouse in a highland landscape on this single-trigger 20-bore by Hartmann and Weiss.

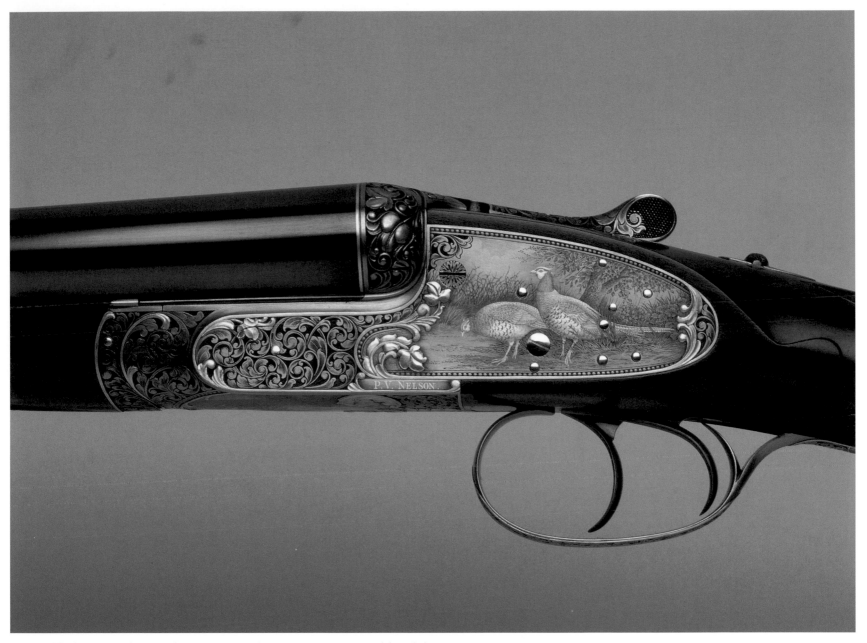

Flat-gold pheasant inlays on this Peter V. Nelson game gun engraved by Phil Coggan.

The underside of the Coggan-engraved Nelson gun shows the lek behavior of prairie chickens.

Woodcock by Alan Brown on the underside of this Hartmann & Weiss.

A bevy bursting from the floorplate of a 28-bore Westley quail gun.

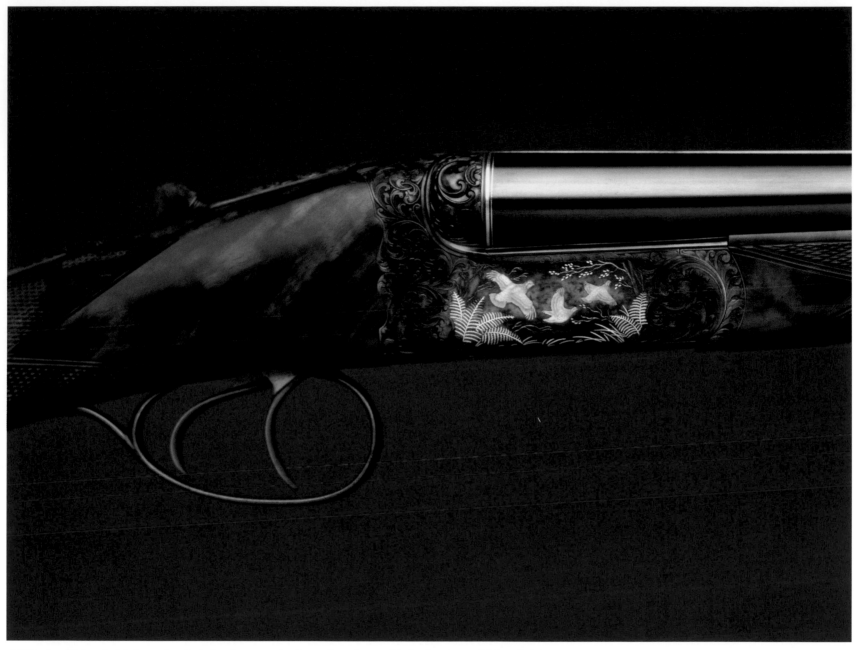

A Westley Richards 28-bore droplock has become the home for a bevy of bobwhites in gold by Phil Coggan.

Golden birds stand out against a color-cased scalloped action.

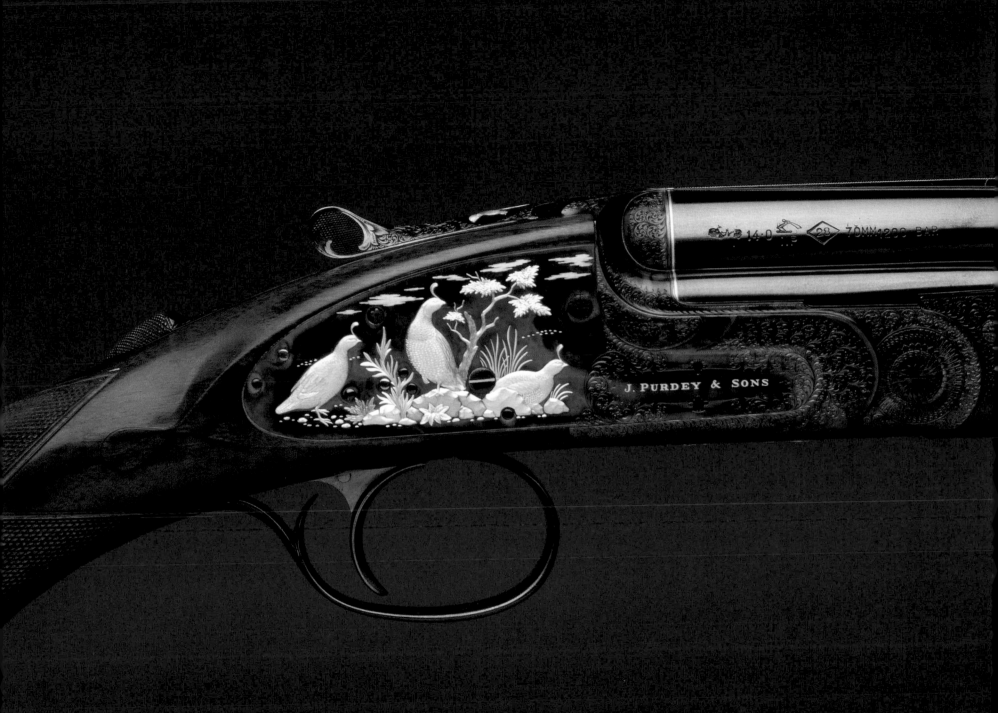

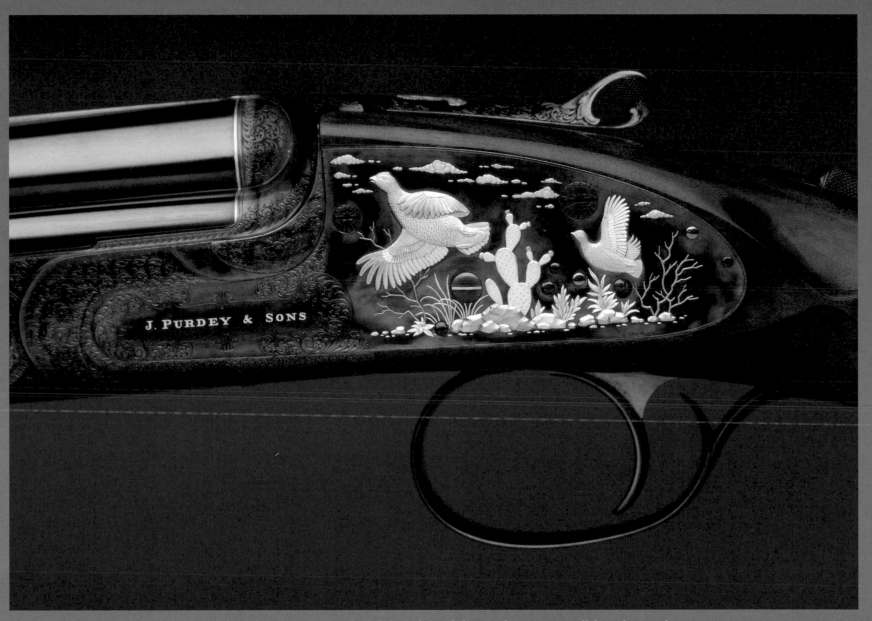

Alan Brown placed these scaled quail in a desert setting on the left lockplate of this single-trigger small-bore by Purdey.

Opposite page: This Purdey two-barrel set (.410 and 28-bore) with a single forearm features California quail in multicolored gold on the right lockplate.

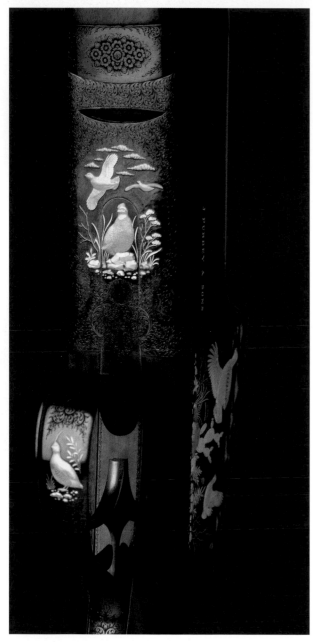

Bobwhite quail featured on the underside of the Purdey over-and-under by Alan Brown.

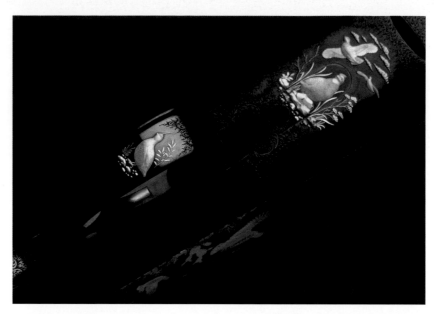

A single mountain quail on the trigger guard of the Purdey over-and-under.

The tiny pistol-grip cap features a portrait of a scaled quail.

Even the Vince Rickard case features a California quail in marquetry by Stuart King based on a painting by Maurice Pledger.

This huge double rifle was given the serial number 29,577 to match its caliber. It is the mate to the Purdey .600 double rifle, serial number 29,600. Engraving by the Brown brothers.

The underside of the Elephant gun from the previous page.

A red grouse bekking on the underside of the Peter V. Nelson grouse gun;
Engraver: Phil Coggan.

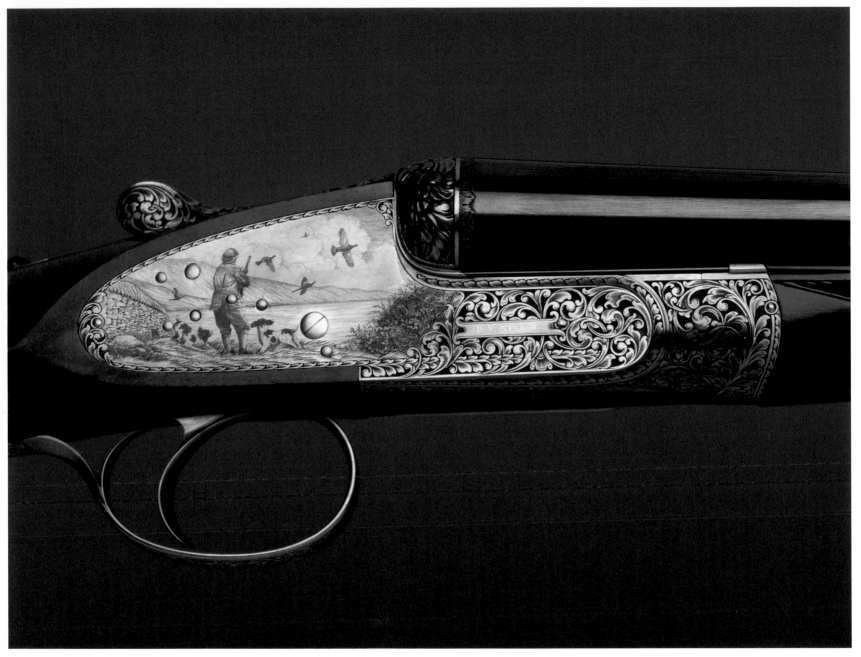

Swerving before the gun. A scene from this Peter V. Nelson 20-bore engraved with a theme of red grouse.

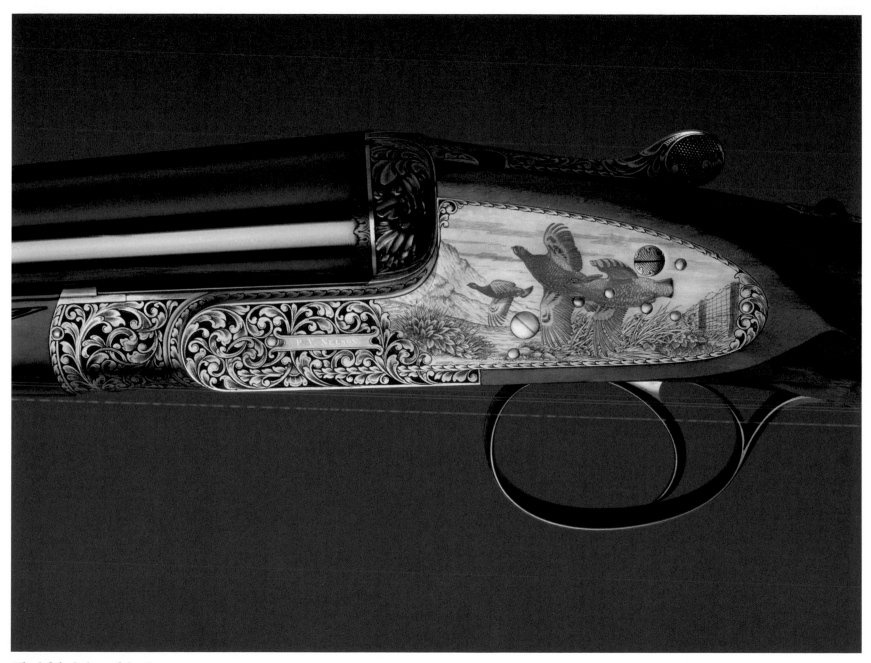

The left lockplate of the Coggan grouse gun.

The right lockplate of this single-trigger over-and-under by Purdey features bobwhite quail. Engraver: Stephen Kelly.

The left lockplate shows a ruffed grouse in flight. Engraver: Stephen Kelly.

Pintails in deep relief on this over-and-under single-trigger 20-bore by Purdey. The engraving is by Ken Hunt.

The buildings in the background of the scenes on both sides of this gun represent actual locations on the owner's estate.

On the left lockplate of this recent H & H the hunter has become the hunted as a pair of Bengal tigers are surprised by an Asian elephant complete with mahout, howdah, and a pair of hunters in sola topees.

Opposite page: In the tradition of a raj rifle, the right lockplate of this modern .577 Rewa-caliber double rifle by Holland & Holland features deep relief carving of a tiger hunting axis deer while a solitary peacock perches on the hinge pin. The work is signed by Paul Brown.

The narrative concludes on the underside with the death of the tiger, no doubt killed by a .577 Rewa. This was a special caliber developed at the request of His Highness Martand Singh, the Maharaja of Rewa, by Holland & Holland in 1921. At the time the biggest double rifle made was the .600 Nitro, which was necked down to .577 with a 750-grain bullet and 110 grains of cordite. The result improved ballistics, impact, and penetration. The maharaja shot more than 600 tigers, which he stalked on foot, disdaining the traditional howdah.

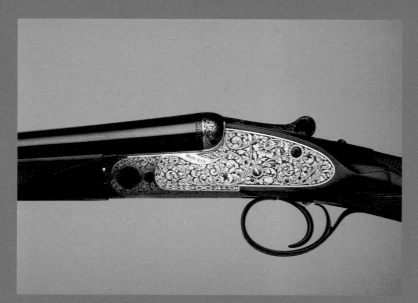

One of a trio of single-trigger .410s by Boss with conventional body.

Another of the Boss .410 trio, this one with a signature rounded body.

The last of the Boss .410 trio, this time an over-and-under. Ken Hunt engraved all three guns in the same style.

English partridge in relief against a matte ground. The same background technique is employed at the base of the barrels. Engraver: Ken Hunt.

Ken Hunt's work on the underside of this deep-relief Rigby.

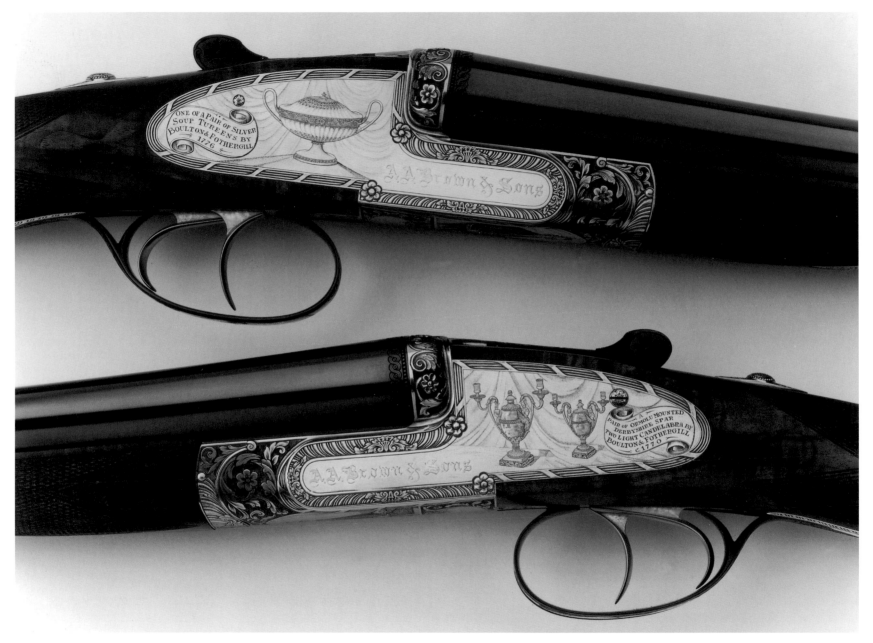

These A. A. Brown guns were created as a tribute to Birmingham's most famous silversmith, Mathew Boulton. Keith Thomas did the exceptional gold inlay.

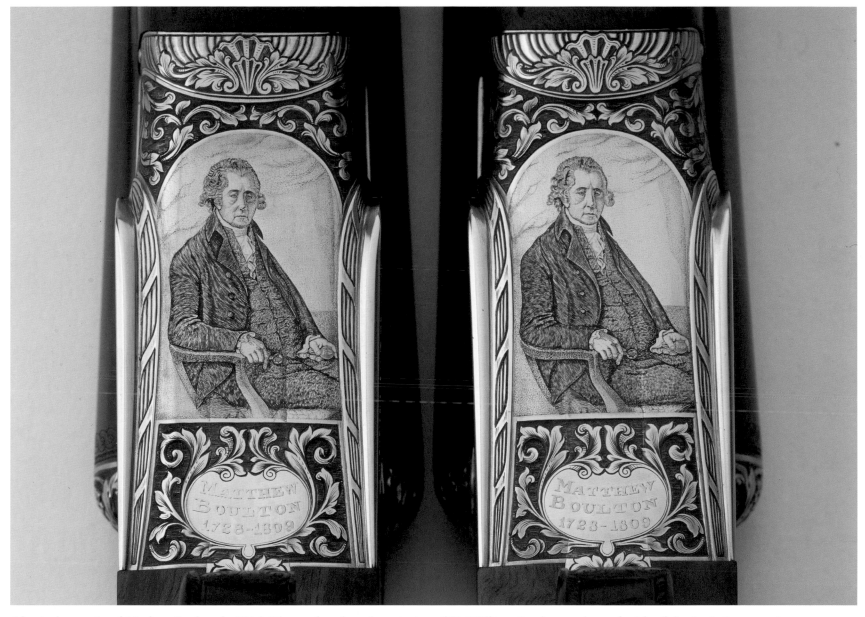

Identical portraits of Mathew Boulton by Keith Thomas based on the painting of Sir William Beechey on the underside of the A. A. Brown pair.

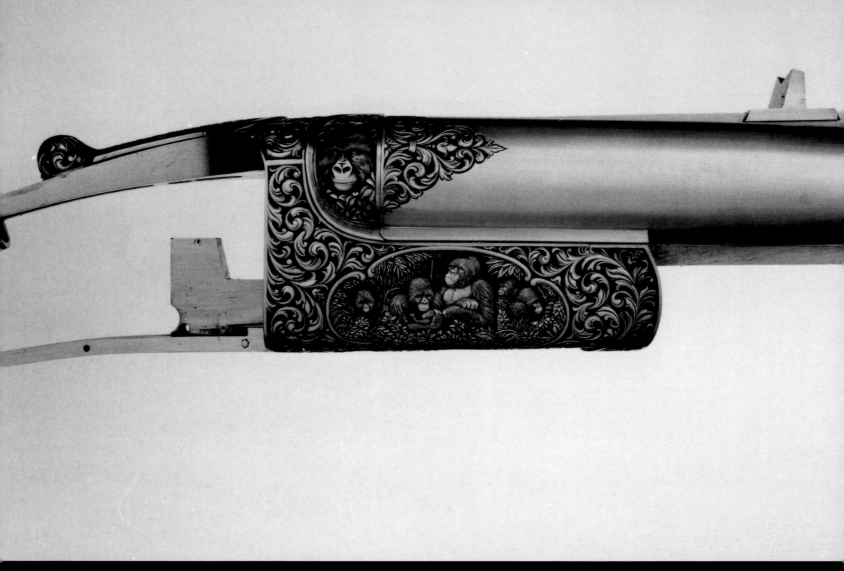

The mountain gorilla double rifle by Westley Richards in .600 with a vignette of the whole family on the action. (Photo: Brown brothers)

The cover plate of this droplock by Westley Richards with engraving by the Brown brothers shows an old silverback becoming irate. (Photo: Brown brothers)

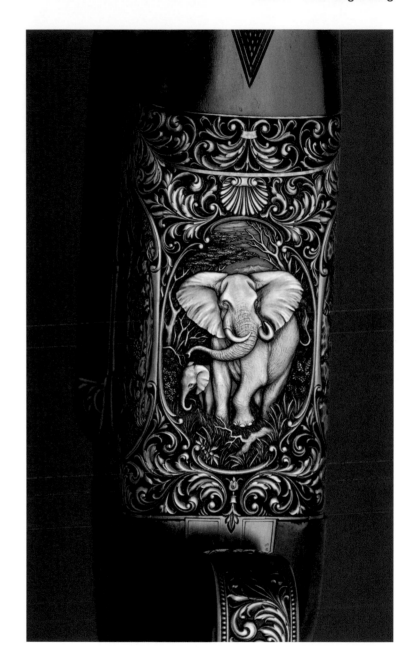

Cape buffalo. Rhino. Elephant on a Westley Richards .600 double rifle engraved by the Brown brothers.

The modern W. W. Greener St. George gun engraved by the Brown brothers.

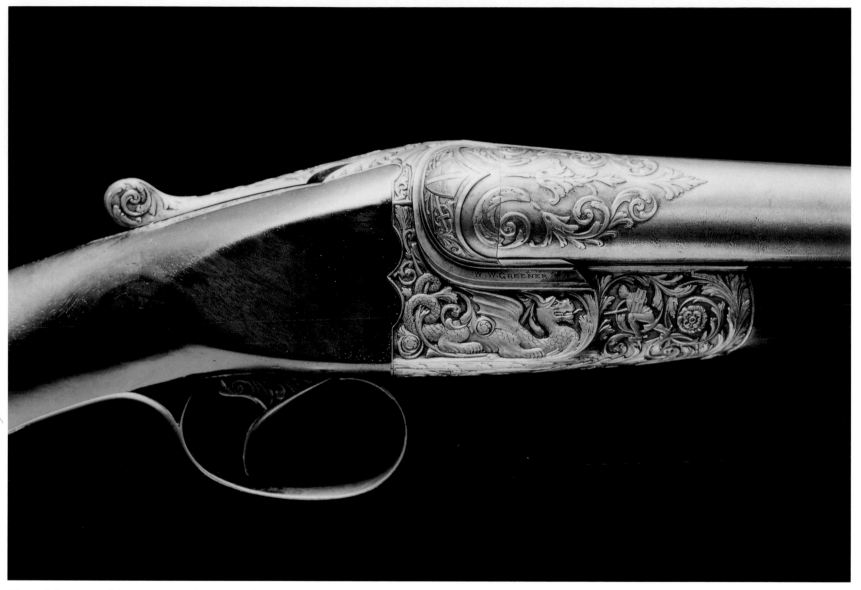

One of the original St. George-grade guns with engraving by Harry Tomlinson from designs by Harry Greener. Built on the "unique" system originated by J. V. Needham, this boxlock was offered in Greener catalogues, circa 1918, for £125. Best pattern London-style sidelock guns sold for £94.10 in the same catalogue.

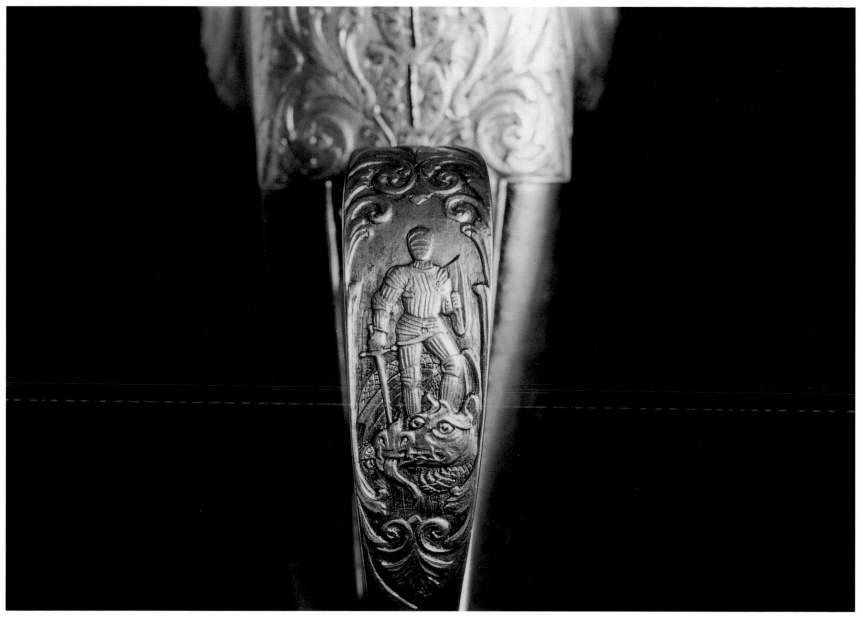

Detail of the trigger guard shows "St. George for Merrie England," as a contemporary Greener catalogue would have it. It went on to say, "No better allegorical slogan could be chosen to typify the superiority of the Greener all-British-made gun." (Ironically, St. George was a soldier of the imperial Roman army who probably originated in what is now Libya.)

It is impossible to say if the game scene and close English scroll featured on this rifle were completed in Britain or if the decoration was executed on the Continent in the English style. (Photo: Tim Crawford)

Opposite page inset: The stag on the underside could have originated anywhere, but the tiger and snake on the trigger guard possess some elements of the Kell school.

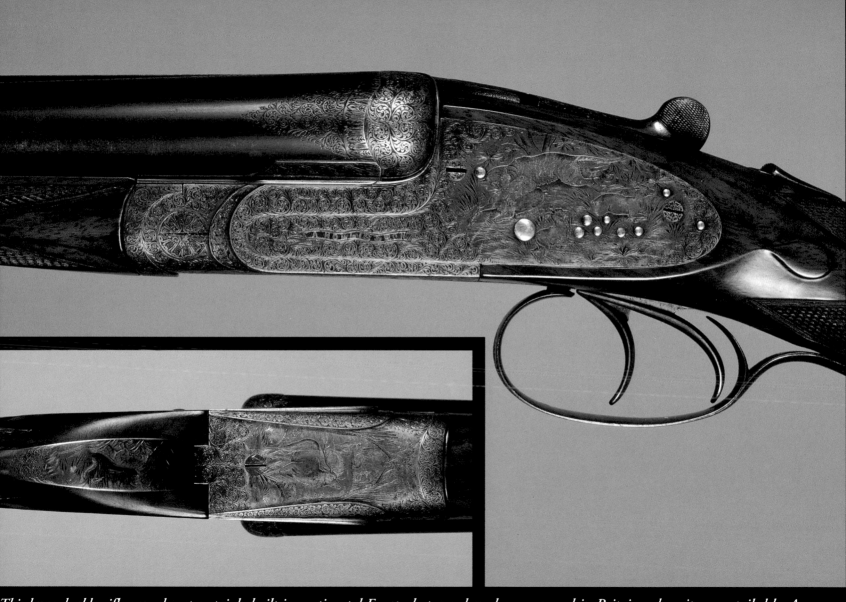

This large double rifle was almost certainly built in continental Europe but may have been engraved in Britain, where it was retailed by A. Hollis of 28 Victoria Street, London. (Photos: Tim Crawford)

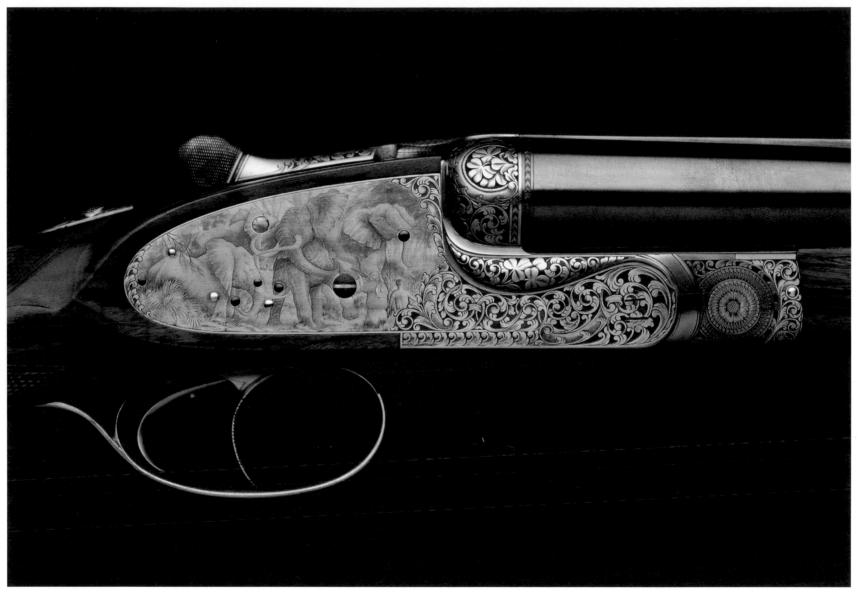

The .500-465 Nitro Express Holland & Holland "Royal" double-barreled ejector rifle with scenes from the life of John "Pondoro" Taylor by Phil Coggan.

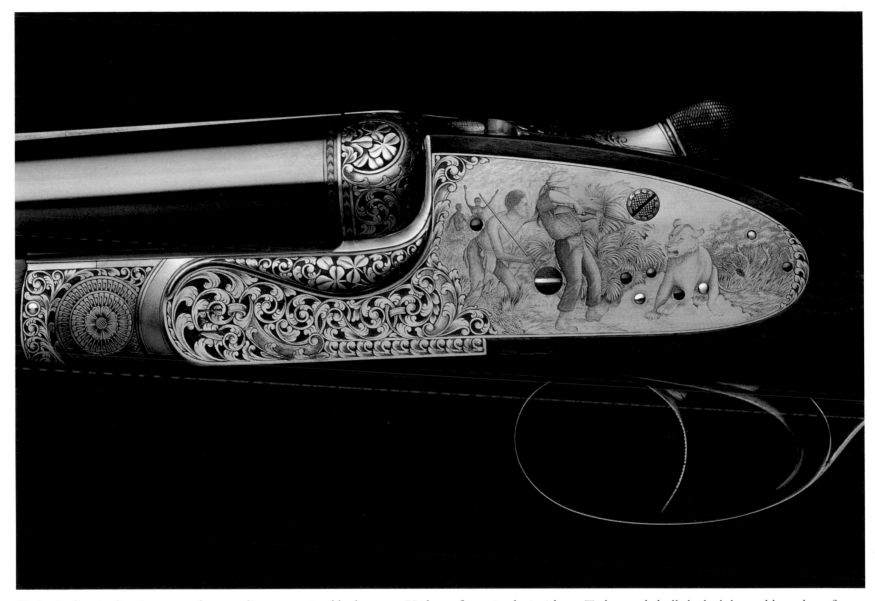

Taylor in favorite hunting gear takes on a lioness at point-blank range. He lost a finger in the incident. Taylor needed all the luck he could get, but of course he was Irish—which accounts for the shamrocks on fences and bolster.

The underside is engraved from a portrait photograph of Taylor.

The pistol-grip cap on the Taylor rifle.

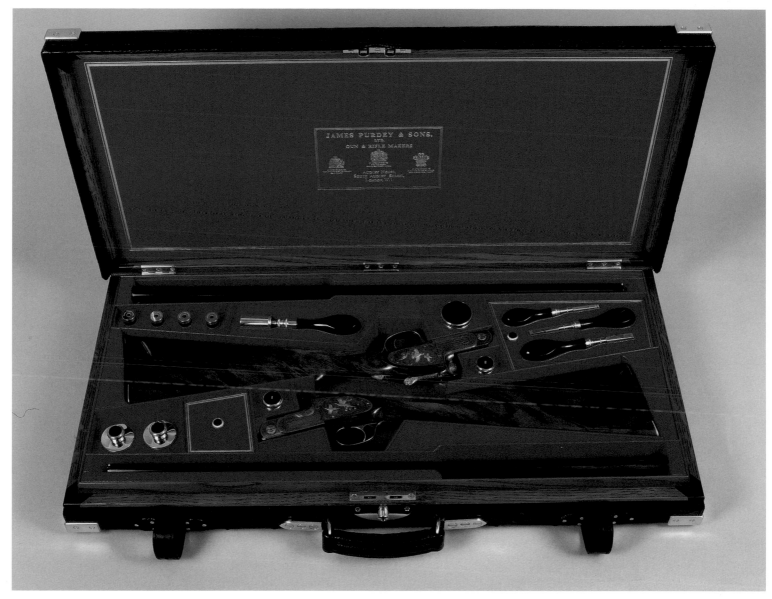

A pair of 20-bore Purdeys appropriately cased by Vince Rickard with all accoutrements. The oak frame is covered with ostrich skin.

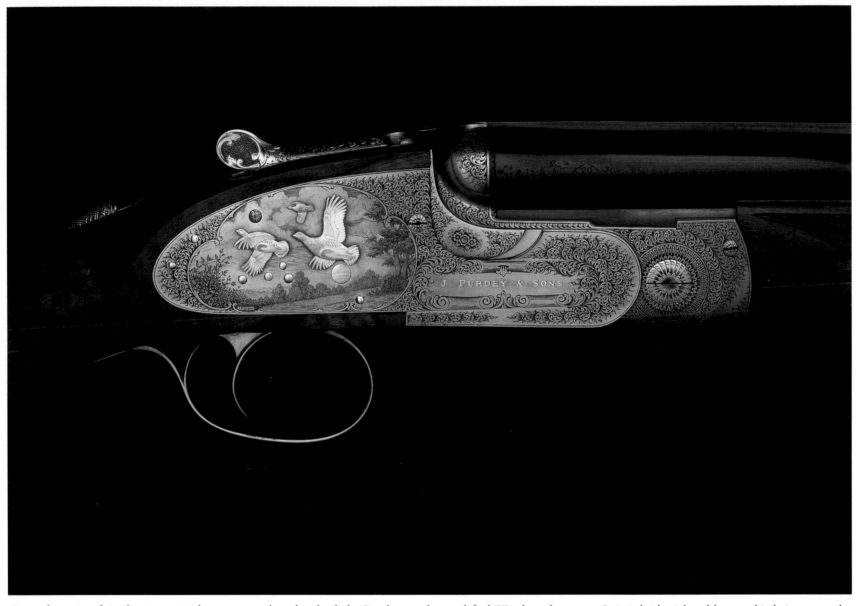

One of a pair of single-trigger 20-bore over-and-unders built by Purdey on the modified Woodward system. It is inlaid with gold game birds in cartouches enclosed by close English scroll. Engraving was by the Brown brothers.

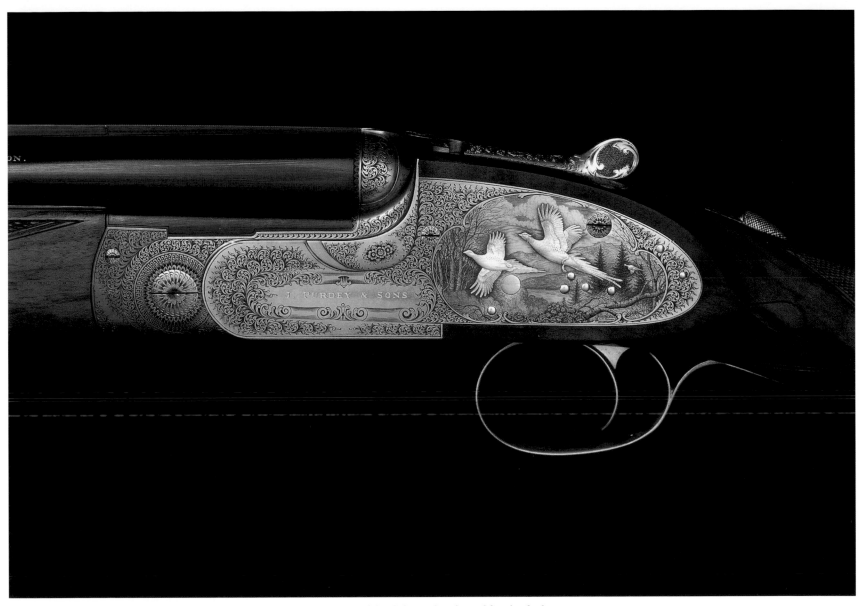

The second gun is similarly engraved with bank note-style engraved backdrops for the gold-inlaid pheasants.

One of a pair of guns that Holland & Holland displayed at the Paris Exhibition of 1900. Although the game scene is clearly inspired by Archibald Thorburn, H&H has no record of who the engraver was.

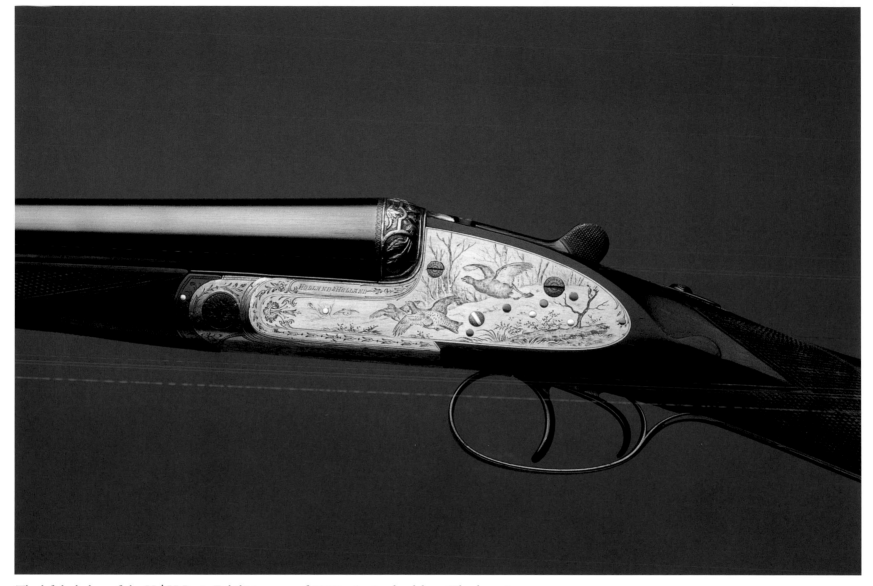

The left lockplate of the H&H Paris Exhibition gun of 1900. Again the debt to Thorburn is apparent.

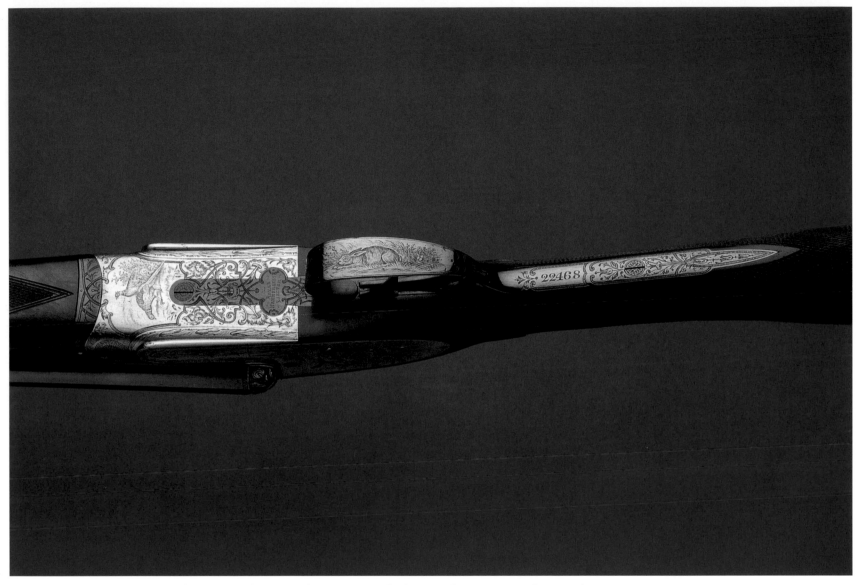

The underside of the Paris Exhibition "Royal Hammerless Ejector." The hare on the trigger guard is superb.

Opposite page: The bevy of bobwhite exploding on the underside of the 28-bore Purdey is vaguely reminiscent of Audubon's Virginia partridge being attacked by a red-shouldered hawk.

Woodcock over the wire on the right lockplate of the 28-bore round-bodied Purdey. Engraving by Phil Coggan.

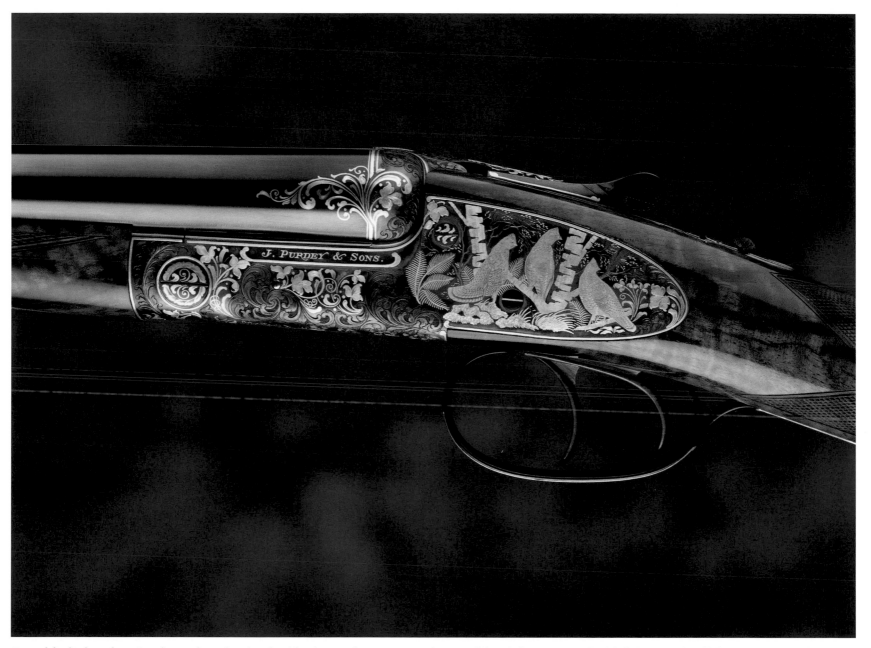

Round-bodied 28-bore Purdey with multicolored gold inlays and museum-quality wood by Phil Coggan. The lek behavior of ruffed grouse among the birches is shown on the left lockplate.

An early commission for the Brown brothers, this Westley Richards in the style of Nicholas Noel Boutet, Arquebusier du Roi, *helped establish the engravers' reputation.*

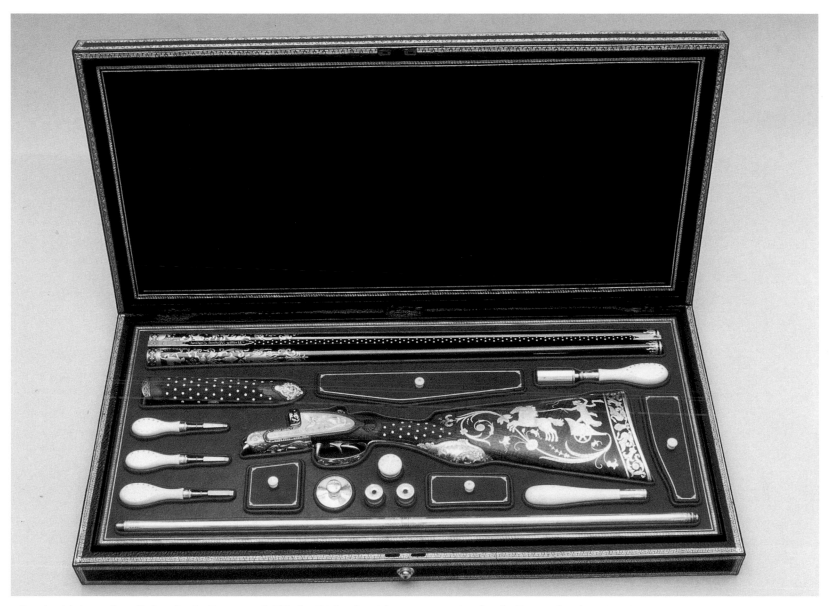

Cased with ivory-handled tools, the Boutet-style Westley Richards with ornamentation by the Brown brothers is unique.

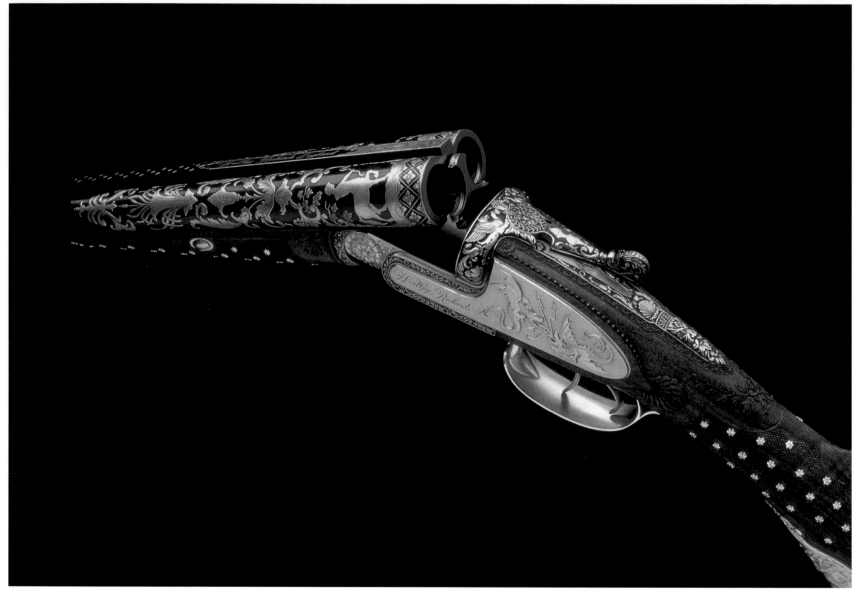

Although it contains all the stylistic elements of Boutet guns seen by the Browns in the Wallace collection, this Westley does not exhibit the aesthetic continuity and wholeness of the brothers' more mature work.

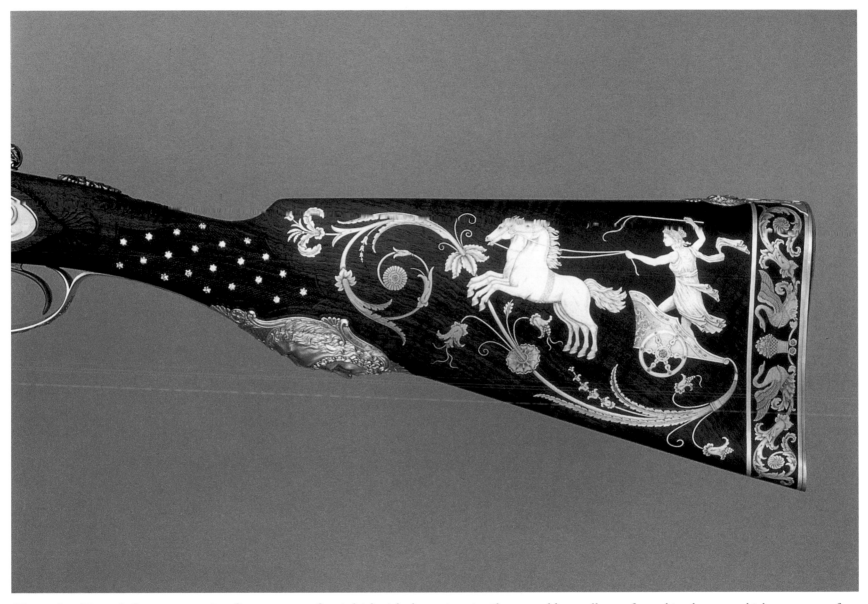

The stocks of Boutet's finest presentation firearms were often inlaid with decorations in silver or gold, usually cut from thin sheet on which ornaments from classical models could be engraved. Engravers: Brown brothers.

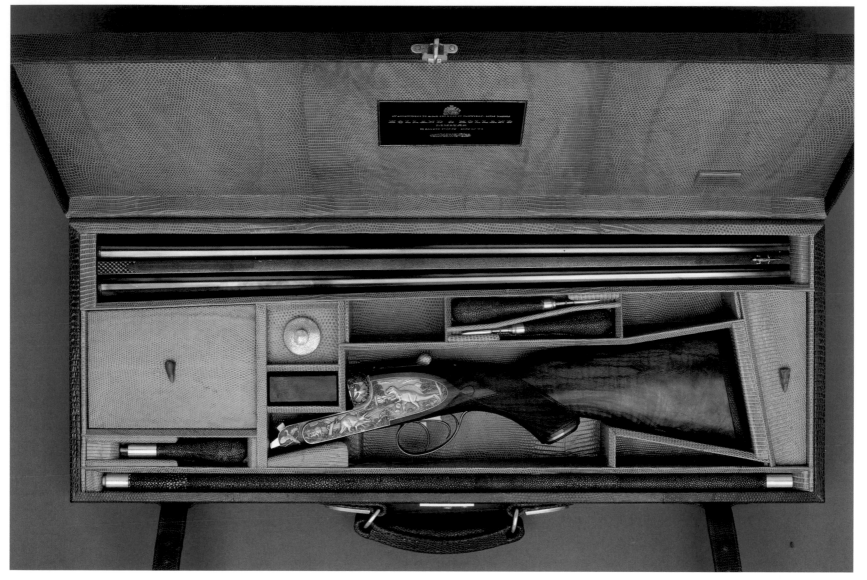

The Holland & Holland Saurian 4-bore with engraving by Paul and Alan Brown. Note the Spinosaurus *and* Triceratops *carved against a backdrop of appropriately Cretaceous vegetation as well as the proto-game bird* Archaeopteryx *on the knuckle. (Photo: Butterfield & Butterfield)*

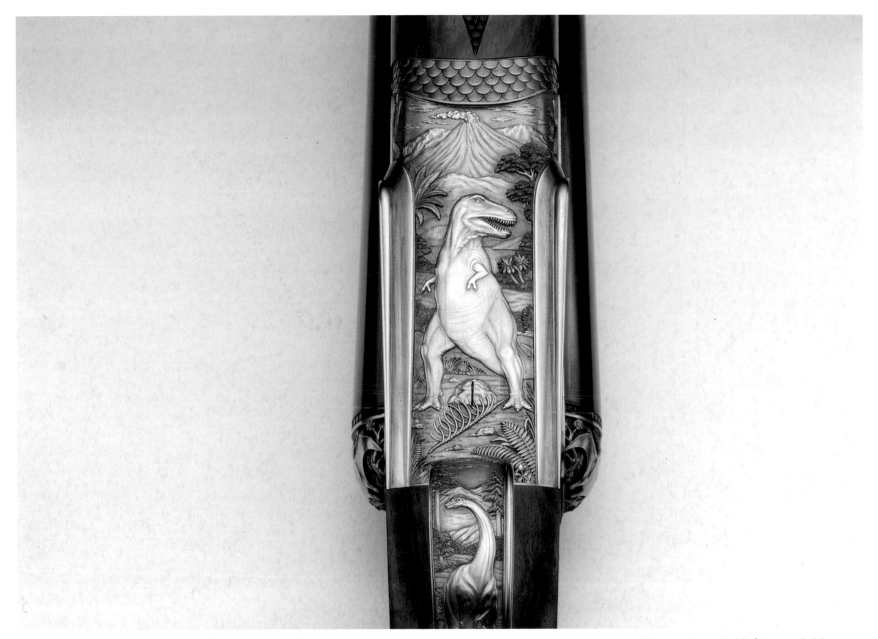

A Tyrannosaurus rex *struts his stuff on the underside of the action, while* Brachiosaurus *guards the trigger guard. (Photo: Butterfield & Butterfield)*

The left lockplate of this Holland & Holland is engraved with a male and female pair of mandarin duck reminiscent of the Japanese woodblock of Utamaro. It is the work of Ken Preater, head of the H&H engraving department.

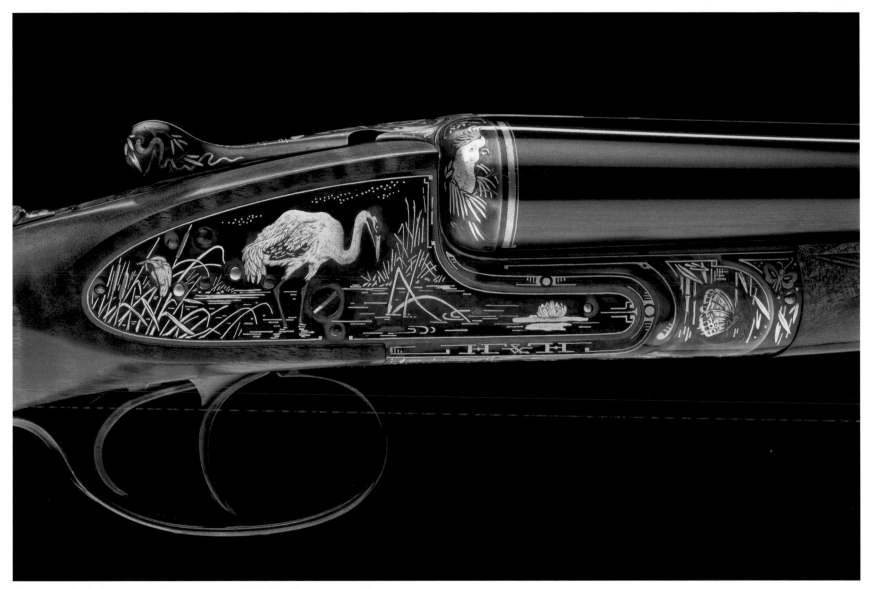

The right lockplate on the Preater-engraved H&H features a wading crane.

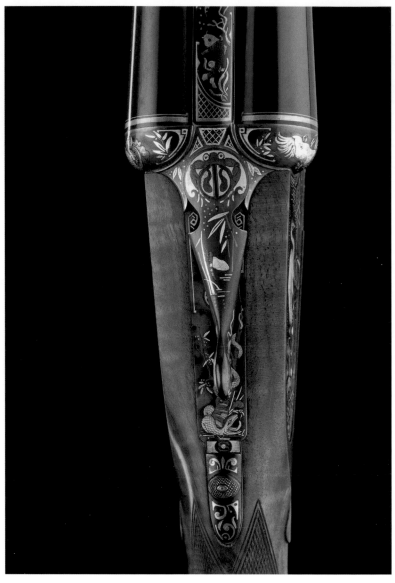

The oriental theme continues on the top of this H&H gun by Ken Preater.

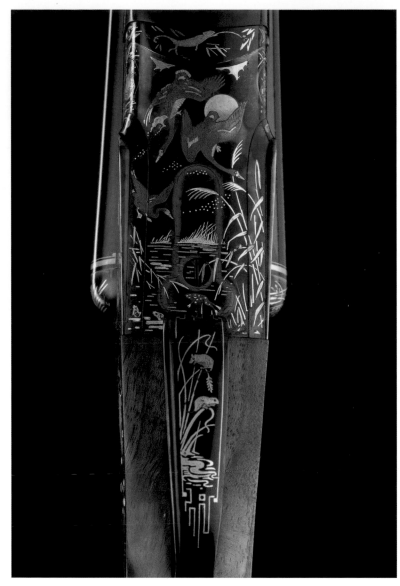

The underside of the action of the H&H appears to have found its inspiration with Japanese woodblock printing. It also recalls a device frequently employed by Audubon: silhouetting his subjects against the sky with only a suggestion of the ground below.

This is the underside of the Holland & Holland swan gun engraved by Rashid El Hadi. It features an egret and bamboo, suggesting the Japanese tradition of bird and plant woodblock engraving.

The Swan gun from Holland & Holland with engraving by Rashid El Hadi was clearly inspired by the woodblock prints of Hiroshige.

On the right lockplate, the perch in the ornamental pool appears to be addressing the mute swan on the top lever.

The Mermaid gun with engraving designed by Malcolm Appleby and executed by Geoffrey Caspard and Ken Preater is one of six commissioned by Holland & Holland on the theme of medieval bestiaries.

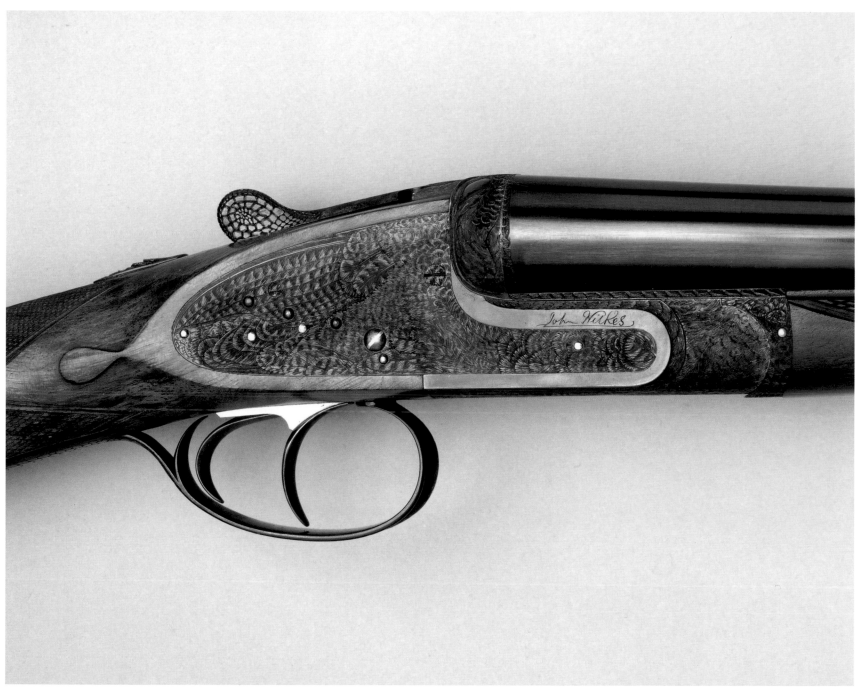

Malcolm's first totum gun was the woodcock gun for John Wilkes. (Photo: Sotheby's)

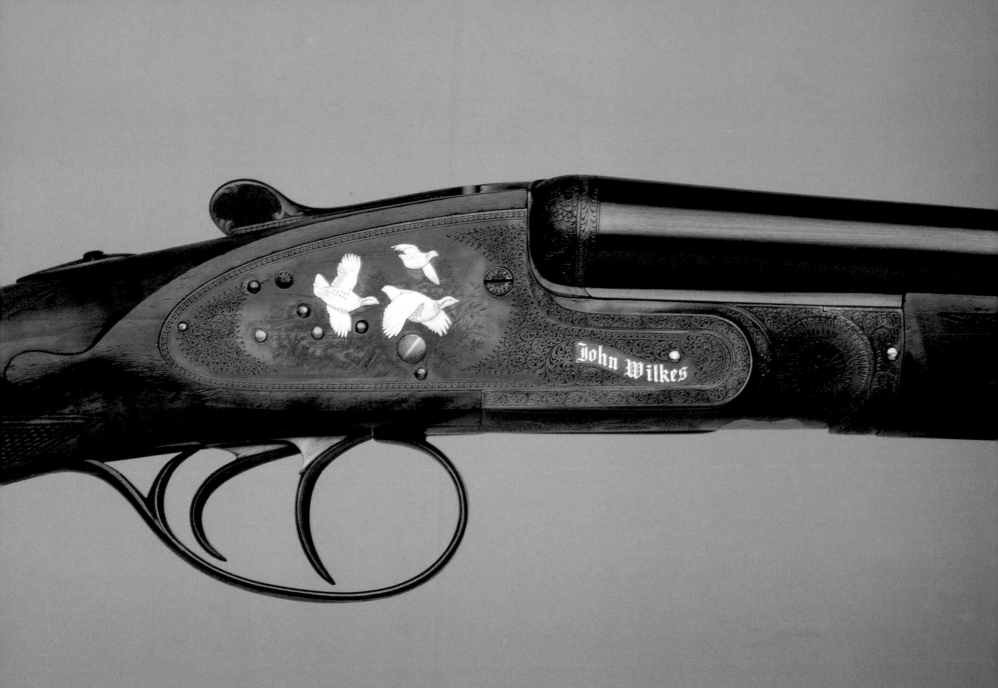

Chapter 8

THE ENGRAVERS

Since the Dunblane massacre, it has been impossible to own handguns in the U.K. However, rifles are still legal and, the laws governing shotgun ownership have been unaffected. The change in the law has had no impact on engravers or engraving because most work done by engravers is on shotguns for the benefit of collectors outside the United Kingdom.

The following is an alphabetic list of British gun engravers. While every effort was made to make it as comprehensive as possible, it is far from complete.

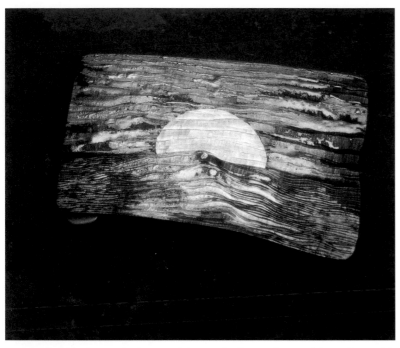

A belt buckle by Malcolm Appleby made from silver, gold, and an old Damascus tube. (Photo: Malcolm Appleby)

MALCOLM APPLEBY

Malcolm Appleby was born in Beckenham, Kent, in 1946 and attended Ravensbourne College of Art and Design. He studied at the Central School of Arts & Crafts while serving an engraving apprenticeship with John Wilkes of Beak Street. It was while he was with Wilkes that he developed the transcendent, totem style of engraving in which birds, reptiles, and fish are not depicted as in conventional game scenes but are represented by their feathers and scales. After further studies at Sir John Cass and the Royal College of Art, Appleby moved to Crathes, Scotland, where he continued totem engraving on round-action guns by David McKay Brown, including the Raven Gun—the first modern masterpiece to be commissioned by the Royal Armouries. Recent commissions have included the design for six Holland & Holland guns based on the medieval bestiaries. He is a Liveryman of the Worshipful Company of Goldsmiths and lives near Aberfeldy, Perthshire, Scotland.

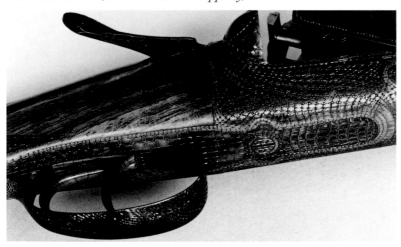

The round action of the crocodile gun is textured to resemble the animal's belly. (Photo: Sotheby's)

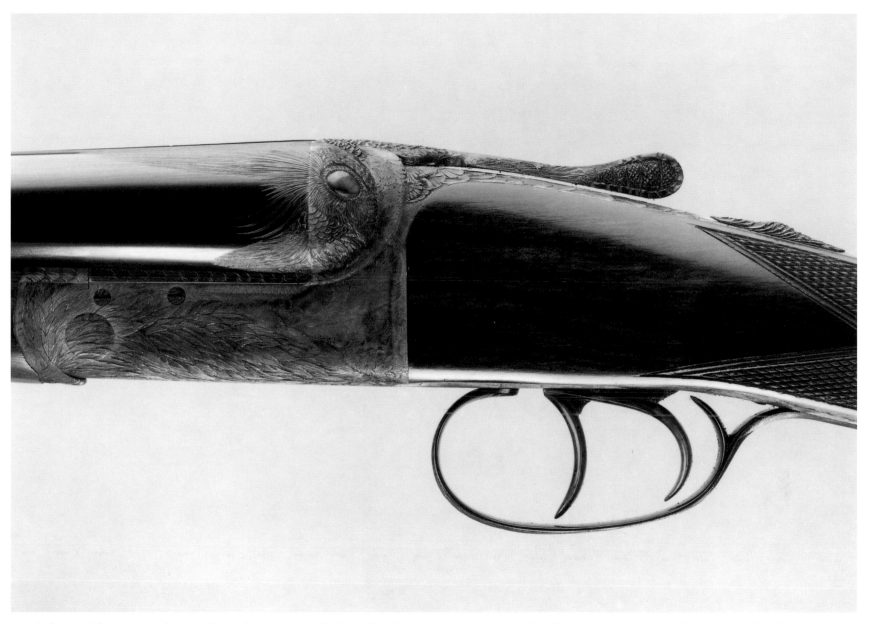

Malcolm Appleby's totem style at its best: the Raven gun by David McKay Brown commissioned by the Royal Armouries. (Photo: David McKay Brown)

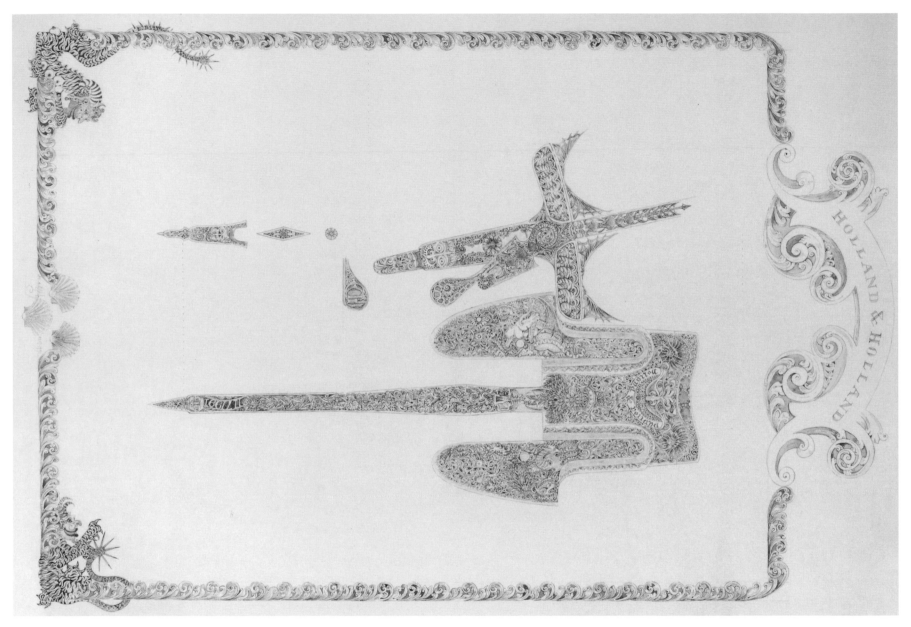

One of the original designs that Malcolm Appleby's executed for the H&H bestiary guns. (Photo: Malcom Appleby)

The pike gun for David McKay Brown is engraved by Malcolm Appleby with the scales of the fish. (Photo: Sotheby's)

The brothers Brown at work in their studio.

PAUL & ALAN BROWN

Paul, born in 1950, and Alan, born in 1954, had the good fortune to be allowed as youngsters to shoot adjacent to their homes. Paul and Alan Brown's interest in engraving developed through renovating their own guns. The chance to apply their newfound restoration skills on fine guns came when a local man allowed them access to his collection. This gave them the chance to examine a wide variety of engraving firsthand. Their early work was sufficiently successful to encourage them to investigate more advanced styles, visiting museums and libraries both in Britain and abroad, and gradually increasing their knowledge of design and technique. Alan turned to engraving full time in 1979, with Paul working at it part time after taking a degree in chemistry.

Their initial goal of creating work the equal of historical engraving was gradually overtaken by a desire to introduce increased realism and detail in their interpretation of figures and decorative designs. After years of experimentation they developed their own tools and techniques, enabling them to advance beyond traditional scroll patterns to more elaborate styles, involving gold inlay, stipple for portraits, and ultimately deep carving. This carving in bas-relief, which is paradoxically minute yet has a monumentality about it, is what ultimately established the Browns' reputation. Although they have mastered numerous techniques, it was their work on the massive Holland & Holland 4-bore Saurian and Herculean guns in 1984 that brought them to the attention of sophisticated buyers worldwide. Such patronage has given them the opportunity to continue to develop and improve their technique—but it has also led to a waiting list of several years.

Brown brothers' engraving is normally restricted to guns, so this knife with peony and "fung huang" engraving is rare.

The medallion on this ostrich-covered case for a pair of Purdey 20-bore over-and-unders was engraved by the Browns.

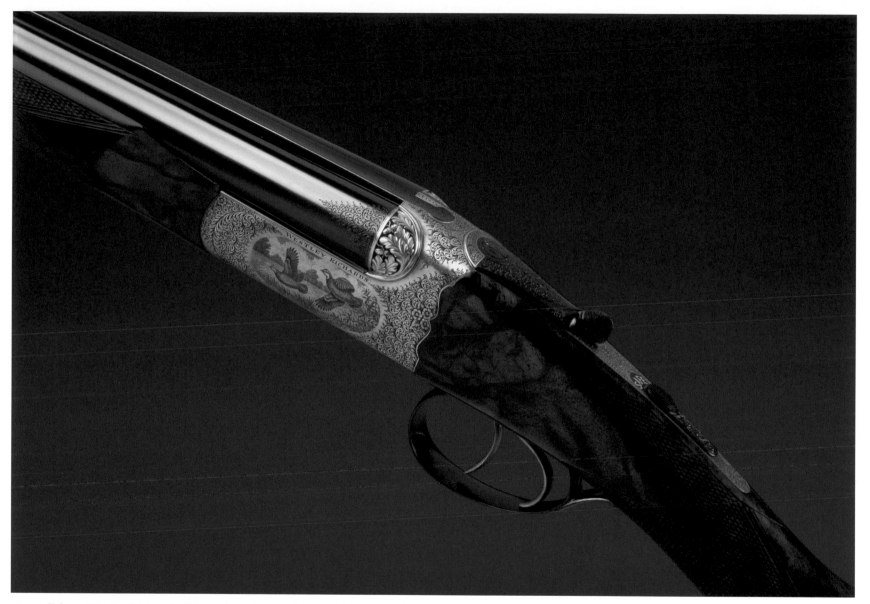

A small-bore Westley Richards, illustrating three techniques the Browns have mastered: traditional bouquet and scroll, carving on the fences, and banknote hyper-realistic game scenes.

GEOFFREY CASBARD

Geoffrey Casbard was born in 1938 in London. His early flair for art led him to the St. Albans School of Art, where he got his first taste of engraving. From there he got a job at Thomas De La Rue, the banknote and stamp makers. He chanced to meet Ken Hunt at the Central School of Arts and Crafts, which they were both attending on day release from their respective companies. It was that encounter that led Casbard to become an apprentice to James Purdey & Sons in 1954.

At Purdey's, Casbard was one of three apprentices being trained by none other than Harry Kell. They worked in a workshop in Soho until 1958, when Purdey's new factory opened at 20-22 Irongate Wharf Road. Kell died in 1958, and the remainder of Casbard's apprenticeship was taken over by Ken Hunt. Casbard remained at Purdey's until 1970, progressing to game-scene engraving and gold inlay. A certain restlessness led him to seek freelance work, of which there has been a steady supply. During his time, Geoffrey has worked for most of the London and Birmingham trade, although recently he has become permanently associated with Holland & Holland. He works from his home and is able to accept commissions from other customers. Only recently has he begun to photograph his work, preferring the more traditional method of ink rubbings.

An engraving of Robert E. Lee by Geoffrey Casbard.

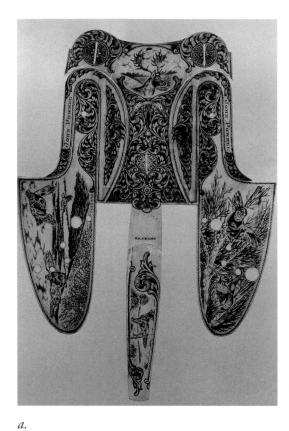

a.

b.

(a, b, c, d). A selection of traditional ink
rubbings from Geoffrey Casbard.

c.

d.

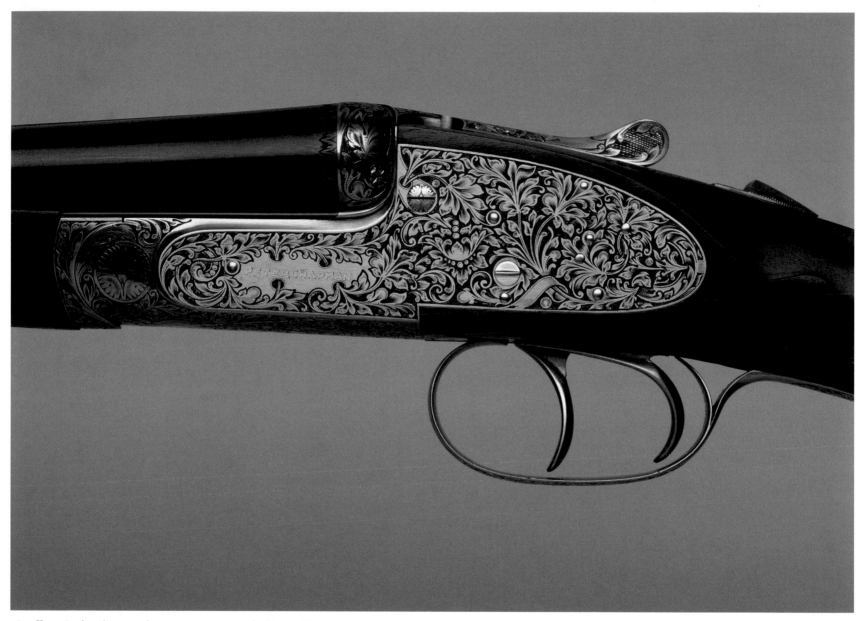

Geoffrey Casbard's acanthus on a game gun by Peter Chapman.

PHILIP & SIMON COGGAN

Born in Fochriw, Wales, in 1948, Phil Coggan moved to Blackpool in the mid-sixties to play lead guitar with a blues/rock band. After a year in the north of England he returned to Wales and became a painter and decorator. In the seventies he made flintlock pistols and muskets as a hobby, becoming interested in the engravings on antique weapons. Unable to find any books on the subject, he taught himself engraving and engraved his first gun in 1984. He became a full-time engraver in 1985.

In the mid-eighties Phil spent two weeks in Gardonne, Valtrompia, with Cesare Giovanelli at his engraving school. Opinions differ as to how much influence the experience had on his style, but what is certain is that he now specializes in portraits and fine game scenes that are more deeply cut than Italian bulino. His work is consequently more vivid, distinctive, and permanent. Today he is more inclined to work with gold and deep carving.

Simon Coggan was born in Fochriw, Wales, in 1970. He worked in the electronics industry until being laid off in 1992. He served an apprenticeship with his father, Phil, starting in 1993 and went full time with his own work in 1994. He works mainly for Purdey and Holland & Holland and lives in Rhymney, Wales.

Phil Coggan at work . . .

. . . and the Purdey double rifle he is carving.

Opposite page: A round-action David McKay Brown with thistles on the fences by Phil Coggan.

The horns of an African antelope appear between stylized acanthus leaves on this double rifle by Phil Coggan.

A leopard digests dinner on the underside of a Phil Coggan double rifle.

Cheetah watch migrating plains game in this bulino scene by Phil Coggan.

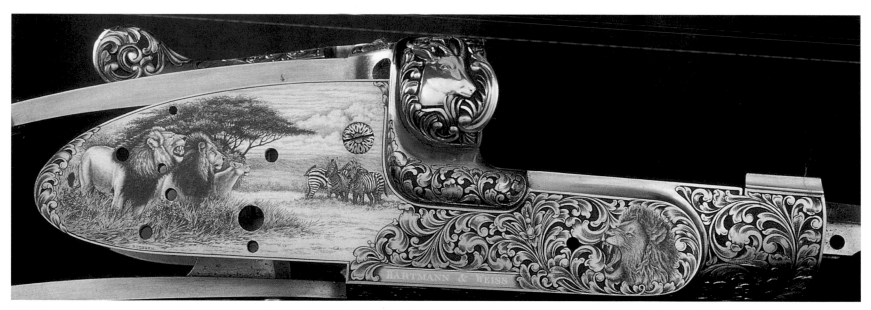

The big cat theme continues on this Hartmann & Weiss double rifle. Note the way in which the bolster and side clips have been integrated into the overall design.

A comic satyr is visible through the scrolling foliage on this gun by Phil Coggan.

Simon Coggan at work . . .

. . . and the Purdey he is working on.

Simon Coggan's work on a Purdey.

Simon Coggan.

Simon Coggan.

Simon Coggan.

RON COLLINGS

Ron Collings began serving an apprenticeship with Webley & Scott under master engraver Walley Howe in 1962. Before completing his time, Ron moved to Wiseman's, then in Price Street, Birmingham, following a row over money at Webley & Scott. Brian Wiseman, who was only a few years older than Ron, allowed him an unusual amount of freedom, and Arthur Evans filed out the mistakes he made, filing out one action so many times that Wiseman's eventually sold it as a lightweight gun. Ron eventually returned to Webley & Scott after they agreed to pay him twice what he was earning at Wiseman's. At the time the engraving shop turned out thirty to forty guns a week, allowing only three to four hours for each model 700.

At age twenty-one Ron left again and opened his own workshop below David Dryhurst on Price Street. At twenty-two he rented space from William Powell, where he continued with trade work as well as working on Powell guns. Two years later he married and moved to Measham. Working from home, Ron did a four-year run of Westley Richards work. It was during that period that he engraved three guns for the Raquel Welch vehicle *Hannie Calder.* In 1980 he moved to California, initially working for Duncans but eventually striking out on his own again. He recently engraved game scenes on the guns Butch Cearcy built for *Jurassic Park, the Lost World,* but he is perhaps better known for the quality of his bouquet and fine scroll. Ron Collings lives in Vista, California.

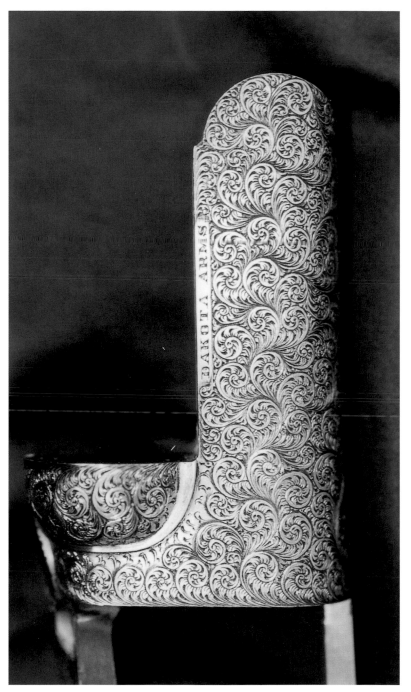

Ron Collings's English scroll.

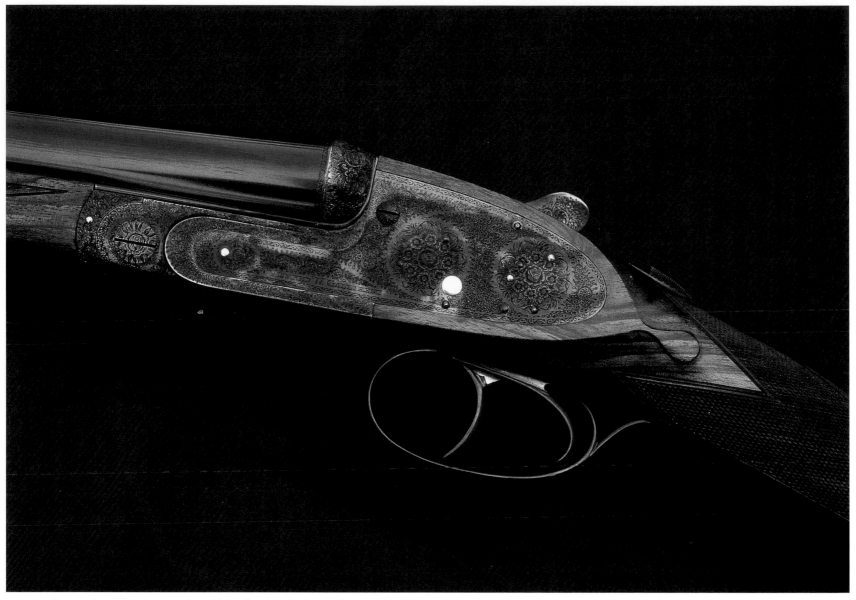

Ron Collings's classic bouquet and scroll lends immortality to this Alfred W. Gallifent sidelock ejector. (Photo: Charles Fergus)

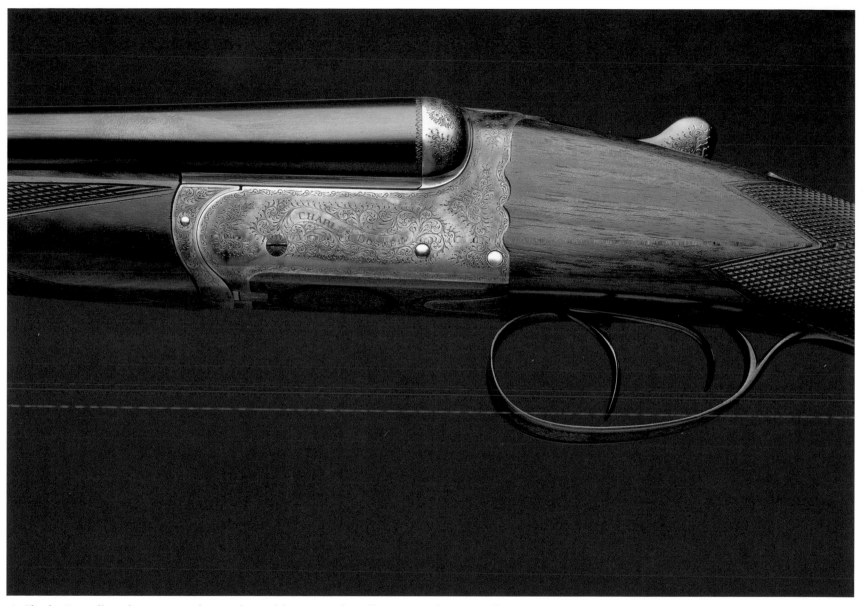

A Charles Boswell 20-bore engraved in traditional banner and scroll engraving by Ron Collings.

PETER CUSACK

Born in London in 1955, Peter left school in 1970 and went to the Sir John Cass School of Art in Whitechapel, East London, to study jewelry. He soon discovered that engraving was of more interest to him, and in 1971 he took an engraving apprenticeship at W. R. Royles, a commercial printer in North London. By the end of his five-year apprenticeship he wanted to undertake more challenging work, and so he applied to Bradbury Wilkinson Banknote printers, part of the American Banknote Company. He worked for Brads for the next ten years until they were taken over by Thomas De La Rue. He was to lose his job again, eleven years later, after having become a top-notch banknote engraver for Harrisons.

It was at that time that he decided to look for a new field of work. Along with doing bookplates and other engraving work, Peter approached Mick Potashnick of the Dorking Gun Company. Mick showed him many fine English guns with impressive engraving. Initially making a few repairs to guns, Peter worked on his first gun in the white after only a few months. Peter's work has come to the attention of Purdey's and Churchill's. With their help, he hopes to move into the premier league of gun engravers

Peter Cusack's work on a recent E. J. Churchill.

Before engraving guns, Peter Cusack worked as a banknote engraver. Here are some of the notes he worked on.

VINCENT CROWLEY

Born in 1977, Vincent had early aspirations to engrave guns. He initially studied at the Birmingham School of Jewelry, where he won the school prize. After two years in the jewelry quarter, he approached Westley Richards. Following some initial trial plates, he was placed under the part-time tutorship of Peter Spode. In 1997 an opportunity arose for full-time employment that coincided with the employment of the world-renowned engraver Rashid Hadi. Under the expert guidance of both Peter and Rashid, he has developed his engraving capabilities considerably and is currently undertaking fine scroll, game scenes, and flush-gold inlay work.

DAVID HUDSON

David Hudson was born in Sheffield in 1945 and served an engraving apprenticeship between 1960 and 1966. He studied heraldic engraving at the College of Arts & Crafts, Sheffield. He became a freelance firearms engraver in 1970. He lives in Sheffield, Yorkshire.

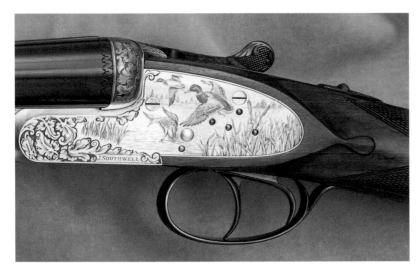

Mallard and stylized acanthus leaf on a sidelock by J. Southwell. (Photo: David V. Hudson)

David V. Hudson at work. (Photo: David V. Hudson)

KEN HUNT, MARCUS HUNT & ALISON BOWLANDS

Ken Hunt was apprenticed at Purdey's in 1950 as an engraver and sent to Harry Kell to be trained. After a short introductory period at Purdey's, his training took place entirely at Kell's Broadwick St. premises. In 1957, Hunt left Harry Kell to do his two years of obligatory military service, and, by the time he had returned, his master was dead.

Initially he went back to Purdey's, but he soon went freelance. He built his reputation by working for Purdey's as well as Holland & Holland and Wilkes, for whom he still works. He has his own private studio in Surrey, where he is joined now by his son, Marcus, and his daughter, Alison.

More than any other engraver, it was Ken Hunt who developed the style of lifelike and artistic engraving. His undoubted artistic skill and liberal use of gold inlays set a new standard that continues to inspire the current generation of engravers in Britain. Blended with traditional English scroll engraving, this new style is extremely popular abroad, especially in America where gold embellishments on fine firearms has long been popular.

Purdey single-barrel trap gun, serial number 27,175, with Ken Hunt's engraving and gold inlay of a thistle.

Ken Hunt at work on a gun for his biggest client.

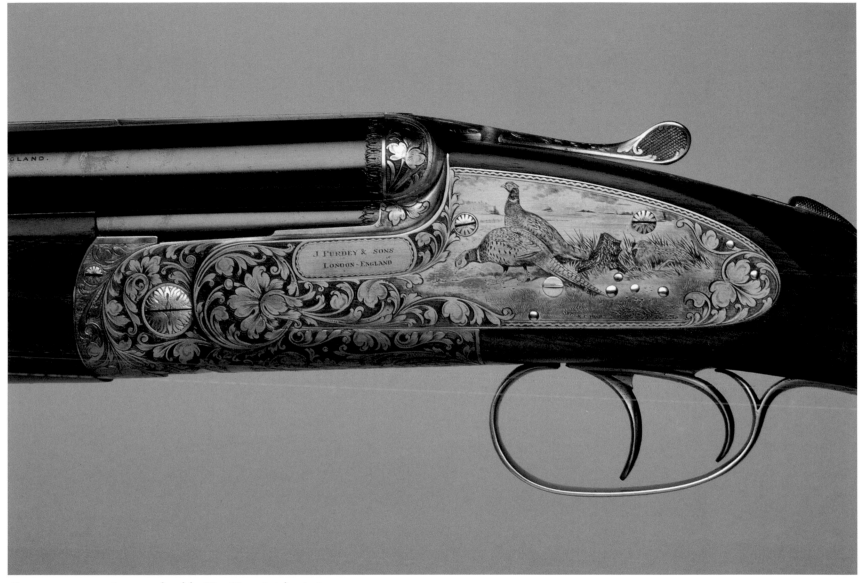

Game-scene engraving completed by Ken Hunt in the sixties.

Opposite page: A 28-bore Purdey, serial number 29,507, engraved with bobwhite quail. The neo-Georgian manor in the background is the gun owner's home. Engraver: Ken Hunt.

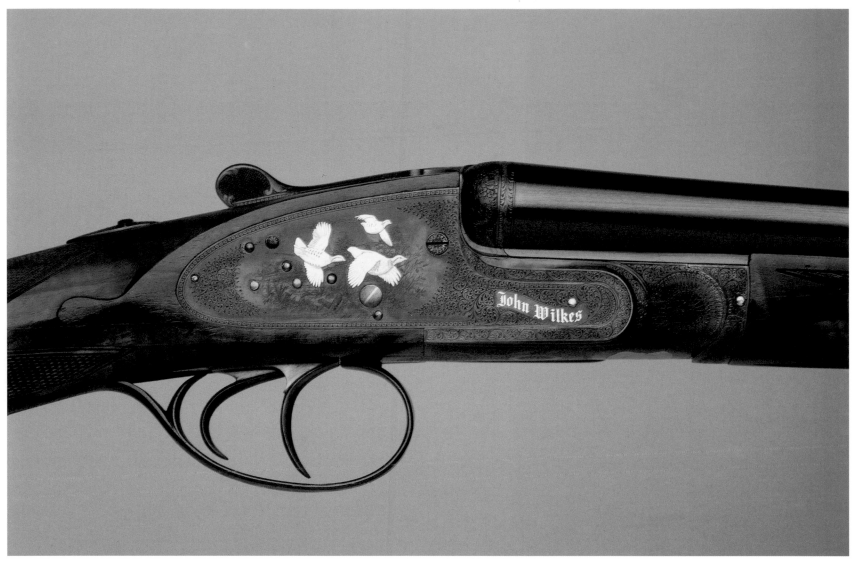

Ken Hunt's gold inlay on a John Wilkes sidelock ejector.

Marcus Hunt's work on a Cogswell & Harrison gun built on the Beesley system by former Purdey craftsman Allan Crewe.

Marcus Hunt's work on a single-shot falling-block rifle in .375 Holland & Holland Magnum.

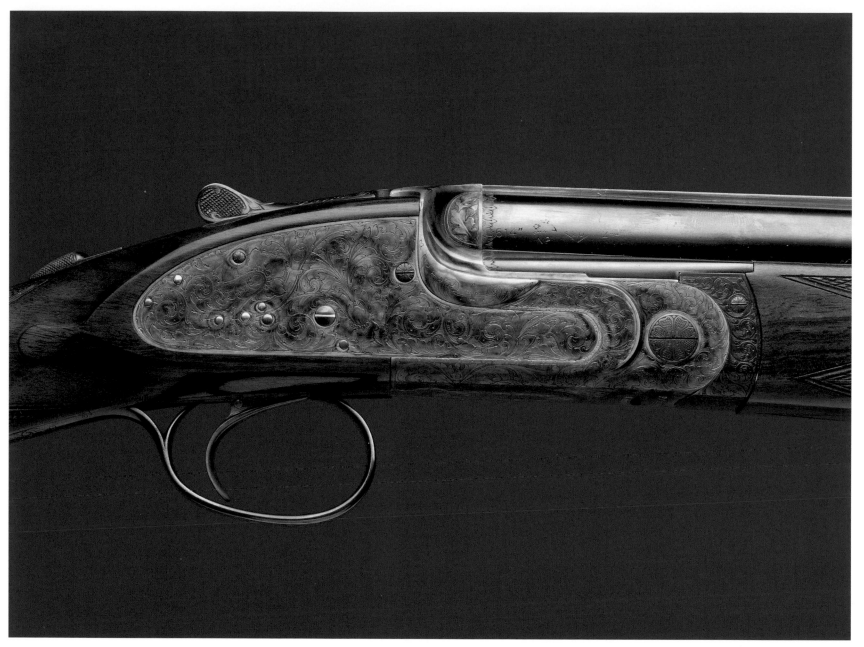

A Peter Chapman 20-bore over-and-under with Brazier locks by Les Arnold, engraved by Marcus Hunt.

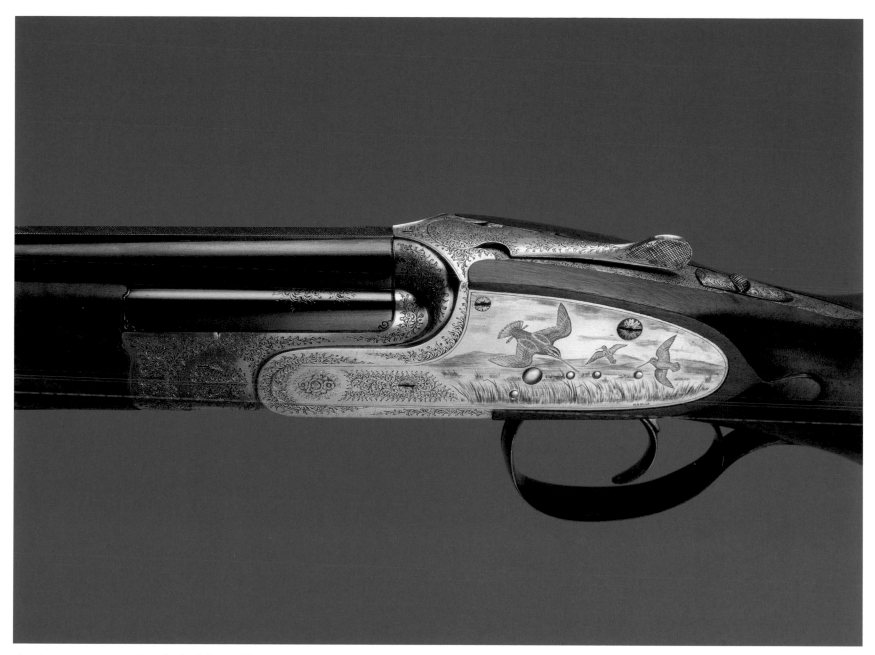

A snipe on an over-and-under by Marcus Hunt.

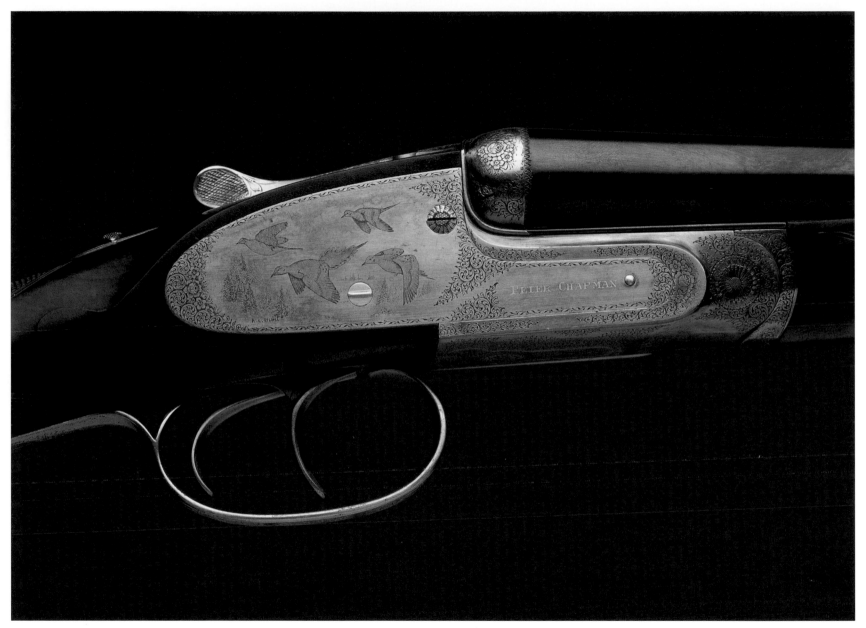

Alison Hunt engraved the doves on this 20-bore by Peter Chapman.

GEOFF MOORE

Geoff Moore has engraved guns for Cogswell & Harrison, David McKay Brown, and Tony R. White. NFIA. I have used the abbreviation NFIA (no further information available.)

A Cogswell & Harrison boxlock ejector with scroll and game-scene engraving by Geoff Moore.

ALLAN PORTSMOUTH

Allan Portsmouth was born in 1963 and apprenticed to Holland & Holland under Ken Preater. He works freelance from his home in Harrow and is perhaps best known for his acanthus work for Asprey. (NFIA).

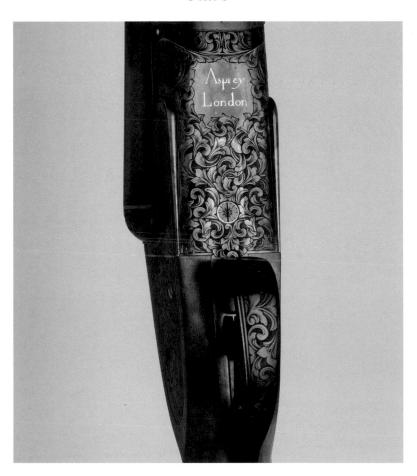

Allan Portsmouth's signature acanthus scroll on an Asprey game gun built on the Holland & Mansfield self-opening system.

ALAN V. POWELL

Alan V. Powell was born in 1934 in Stratford, London. He is a distinguished engraver for many of Britain's top jewelers but has only recently begun to engrave guns. During the last eight years, he has completed work for Purdey, Holland & Holland, as well as many other top makers. He has not had a chance to do much game-scene engraving but works continuously on scrollwork. Alan lives in Stanford-le-Hope, Essex.

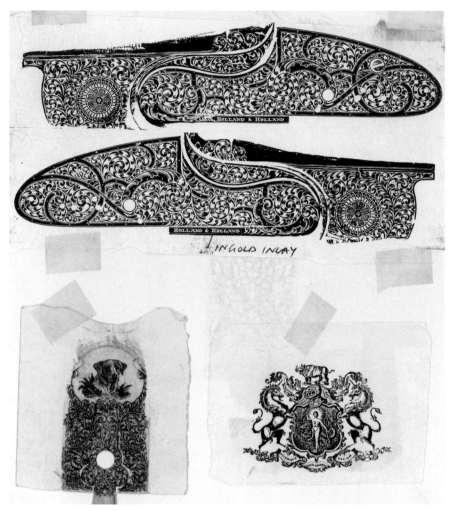

A selection of rubbings from the workbook of Alan V. Powell.

JOHN SALT

Born in 1939 in Tunstall, one of the six towns that make up the city of Stoke-on-Trent, John showed a keen interest and early talent for art. The Junior Art School, an early training ground, accepted him for future designers, painters, and engravers in the pottery industry. Unfortunately, he was unable to continue on to senior school as the death of his father forced him to seek employment. He secured an engraving apprenticeship with a local pottery manufacturer. After ten years he moved south and became involved in many different aspects of engraving, including silversmithing and jewelry engraving. He became a part-time tutor in the Jewelry Department of the Mid Warwickshire College and accepted freelance commissions. About 1986, John started to work for a local gunmaker, Hogan & Colbourne, who imported Spanish actions. This was his first encounter with gun engraving. He has learned by copying the work of long-established engravers in the trade.

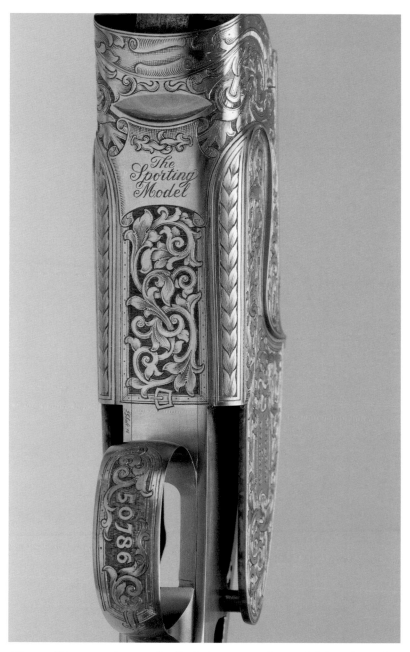

The scrolling acanthus on this H&H sporting-clay model by John Salt is modern but contains traditional elements.

John Salt at his bench. He is working on one of Holland & Holland's sporting-clay guns.

A different take on Purdey's extra finish by John Salt for Holland & Holland.

The underside of the Holland & Holland pair with extra finish by John Salt.

DONALD SIMMONS

Born in 1934, Don spent his early years in the Wembley area. His first interest in engraving came about when silversmithing in art school, which led to an apprenticeship with Holland & Holland around 1950. After three years of service in Germany, Korea, and Hong Kong, he returned to Holland & Holland for a couple of years before moving to Cogswell & Harrison as an engraver. He stayed at Cogswell until 1970, when he went freelance. Since that time, he has engraved guns for Holland & Holland, John Wilkes, Cogswell & Harrison, E. J. Churchill, Westley Richards, Asprey, Hendry, Ramsay & Wilcox, and James McNaughton & Sons of Scotland. He now makes his home in Berkshire, specializing in gold inlay, high relief, and game engraving.

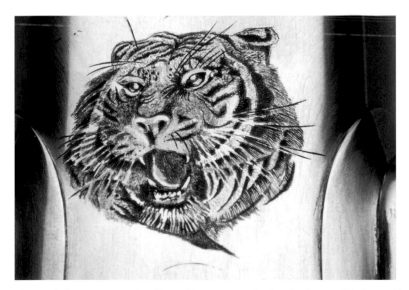

A work in progress by Don Simmons: Left: before. Right: after the scroll has been added.

A lion engraved on the lockplate of an African double rifle for Holland & Holland by Don Simmons.

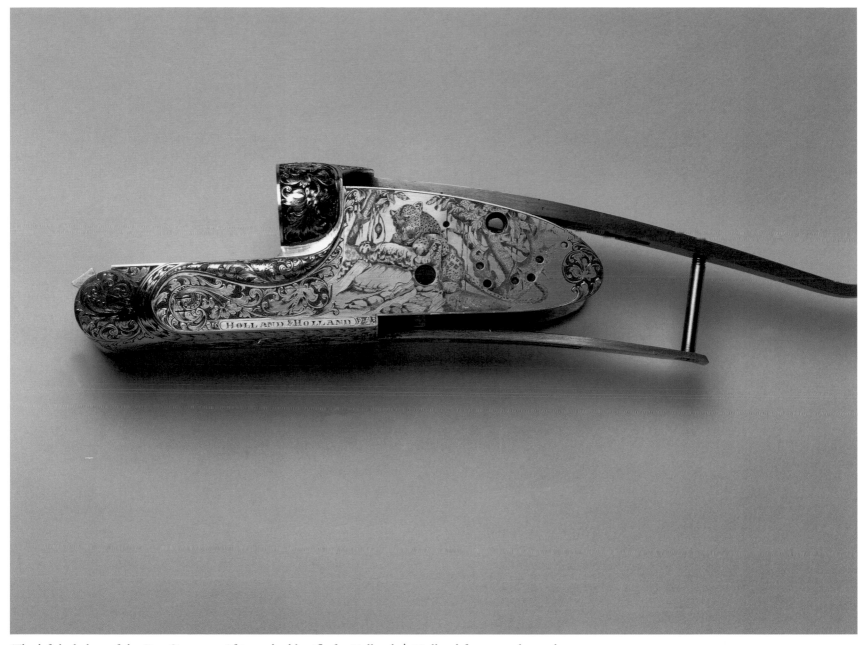

The left lockplate of the Don Simmons African double rifle for Holland & Holland features a leopard.

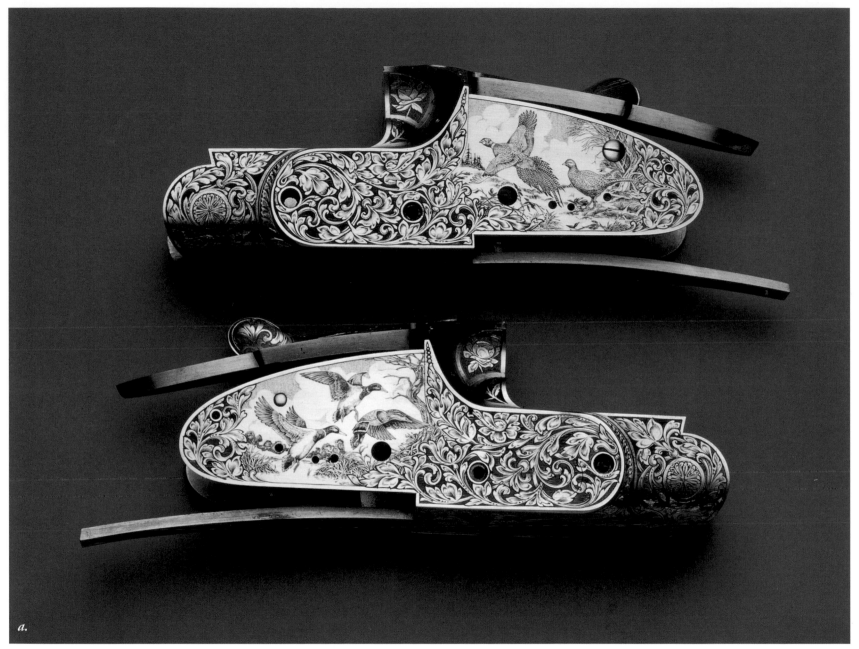

(a & b) Bill Sinclair's favorite game-scene work on a pair of over-and-unders for Frederick Beesley.

W. P. (BILL) SINCLAIR

Bill Sinclair was born in Glasgow in 1936. In 1957, returning from a stint in the Royal Air Force, he joined Alex Martin, the Glasgow gunmakers. After a couple of years he went to London and worked for Cogswell & Harrison, mostly in the front shop, renting firearms to the film industry. He later left Cogswell to operate as a freelance armourer to films.

Over the next few years he worked for Dickson's of Edinburgh, again for Alex Martin, and a second time at Cogswell & Harrison. Self-taught, he first tried engraving in 1971 with the encouragement of Ken Hunt. By 1973 he was engraving complete guns, part time. In 1978 he took the work up full time and moved from London to Wiltshire.

Like many contemporary engravers, he especially favors game-scene work. He is unusual amongst his peers insofar as he had had a broad background in the trade before becoming a full-time engraver. He designed and produced the Loadmaster patent shotgun cartridge dispenser, which is currently available in many countries. The original designs were produced in 1988, and the first production models were available for the 1990 shooting season.

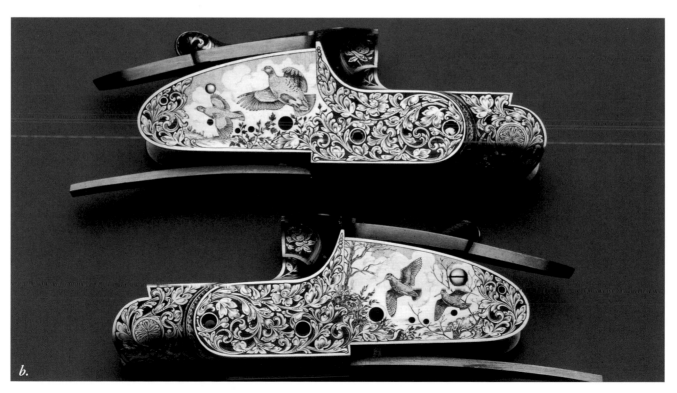

b.

MARTIN K. SMITH

Martin Smith was born in Hammersmith in 1971 and went to school at Gunnersbury. His initial interest in engraving was fired by images in a library book. In 1987 his cousin Michael Smith, a former barrel-filer, introduced him to Rashid El Hadi, and he was inspired to become an engraver. Later that same year he was apprenticed to Purdey's, where he was taught by Martin Bublick. He stayed at Purdey's until 1993. His biggest influences have been Rashid, who Martin says "is unbeatable," and Ken Hunt, the "all-time great"; their influence is obvious in his work. Martin has executed jobs for Purdey's, Holland & Holland, Boss & Co., and David McKay Brown. His favorite media are deep scroll and game-scene engraving. He currently operates freelance out of the Watson brothers' workshop in South London.

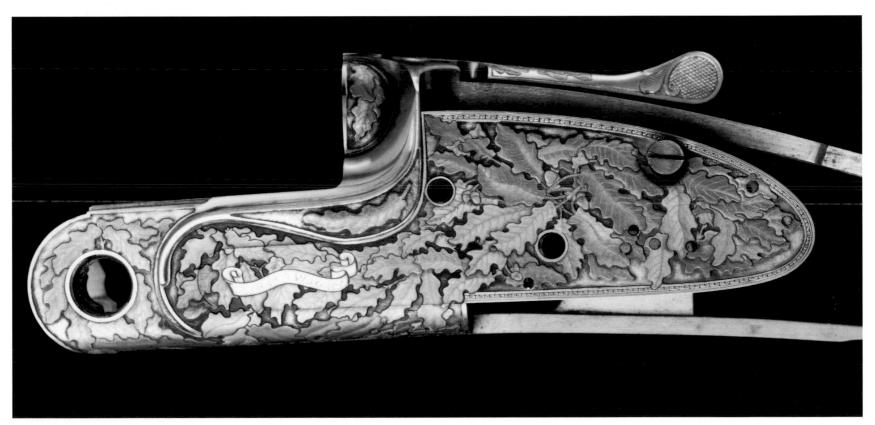

Oak leaf engraving on a Symes & Wright over-and-under by Martin Smith.

Opposite page: Martin Smith's game-scene engraving on the floorplate of a Westley Richards double rifle.

PETER SPODE

Born in 1947, Peter is a self-taught engraver who has worked part time for the last thirty years while pursuing a career in education. During that time, he has worked with scrimshaw, antique restoration, and custom knives as well as gun engraving. Peter has been associated with Westley Richards for the last ten years. He works in all styles and is currently specializing in deep carving and relief work in steel.

BRADLEY TALLETT, WESTLEY TALLETT AND DAVID TALLETT

There are three engravers in the Tallett family. The father, David, had pursued his interest in gun engraving as a hobby. Increasingly frustrated with his daytime job, however, he took his hobby more seriously, engraving some practice pieces that he showed to friends in the gun trade. One of these friends, a stocker, recommended that he show his work to Nigel Beaumont of J. Purdey & Sons, who agreed to take him on as a trainee.

Brad, at that time a teenager, was set to go to art college when he saw a copy of the book *Modern Fire Arms Engraving*; he instantly knew what he wanted to do. He decided to try his hand on a few pieces of copper, which his father, by

then working to a high standard, showed to Mr. Beaumont. In September 1991, Brad began a five-year apprenticeship at Purdey's under Tim Rawson, who taught him standard fine English scroll. In April 1992, his father left Purdey's to work freelance while Brad remained at Purdey's, where he worked on guns and also attended the Sir John Cass School of Art once a week. There he developed his repertoire of game scenes, gold inlay, and large scroll with the help of Wayne Parrott. Brad's biggest inspiration came from the work of Ken Hunt, the Brown brothers, Phil Coggan, and Steve Kelly. At the end of his first year, Brad received two awards from the college in its annual prize presentation, and he went on to win further awards during the next three years.

It became apparent that there was little point in Brad's completing his apprenticeship, as he had already achieved the quality of work expected; furthermore, there was little room to develop his work in the Purdey's workshop. In February 1995, Brad won first prize for engraving in the much-respected Goldsmiths Crafts Council Awards, and in June 1995 he left Purdey's to work freelance. Since that time he has worked almost exclusively on Purdey guns, sometimes with his father, who is now doing work for many of the major British gunmakers.

Brad's younger brother, Westley, started to learn engraving in 1996 after completing a college course in art and design. He is showing great potential, and recently he too has won first place in the Goldsmiths Crafts Council Awards. He has now started as a trainee at Holland & Holland.

Opposite page: The current fashion for deep-relief carving is apparent on the cover plate of this Westley Richards heavy double rifle by Peter Spode.

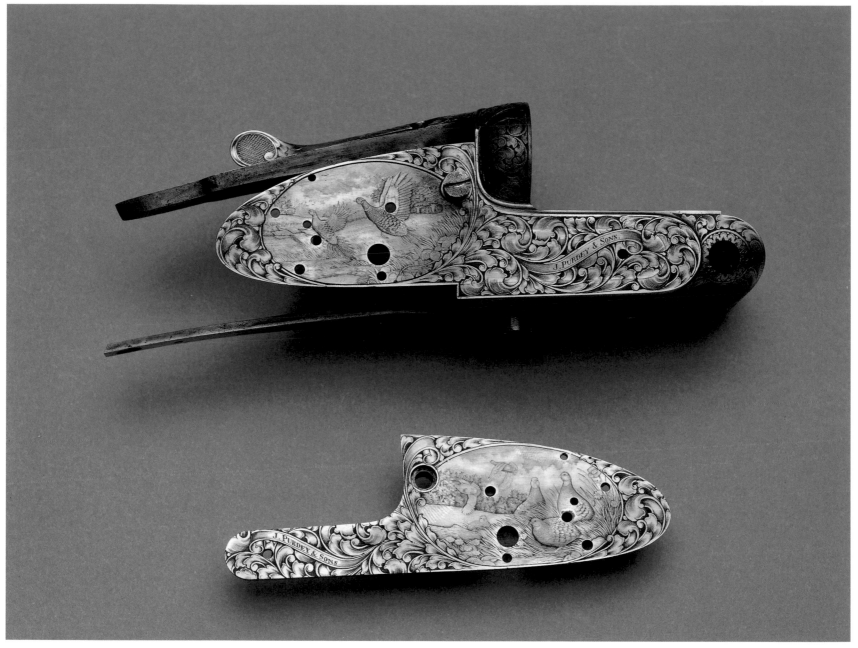

Game scene within vignettes on a side-by-side game gun by Purdey. The engraver is Brad Tallett.

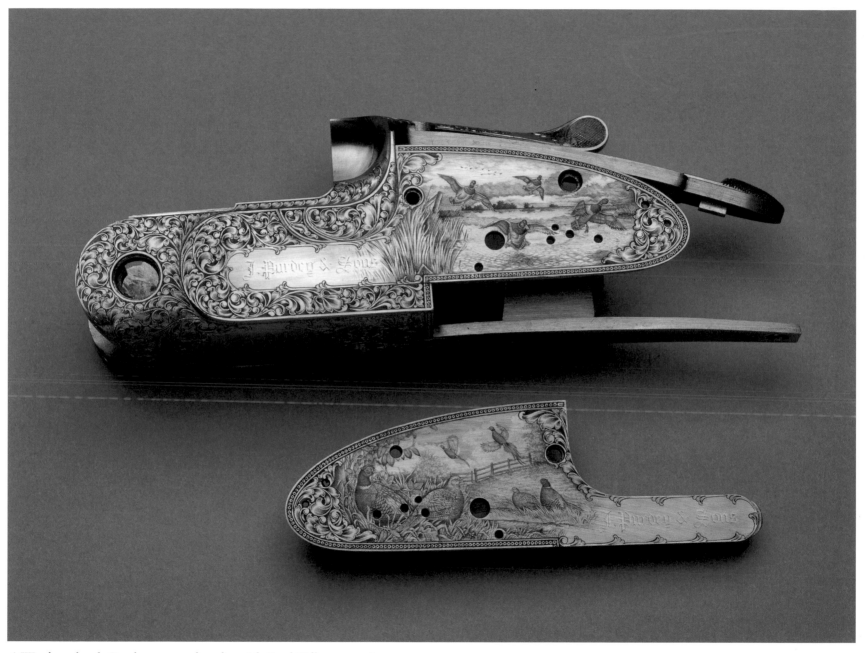

A Woodward-style Purdey over-and-under with Brad Tallett engraving.

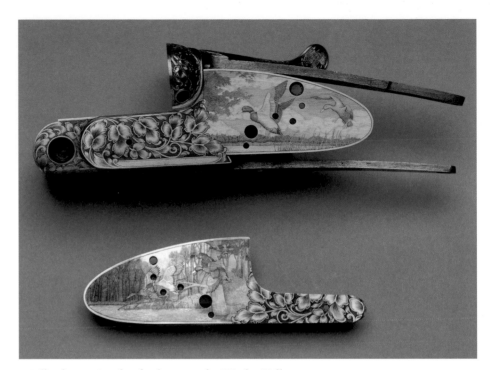

Mallard on a Purdey fowling gun by Westley Tallett.

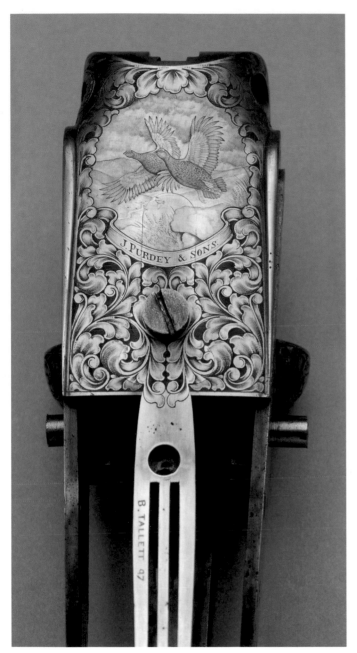

A brace of airborne grouse by Brad Tallett on the underside of a Purdey.

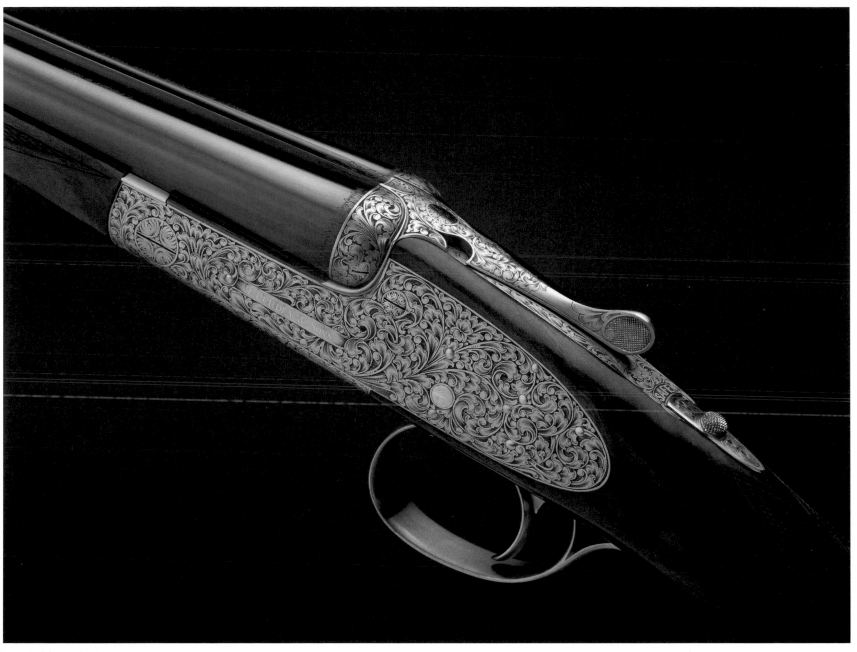

Brad Tallett's interpretation of Purdey's extra finish.

KEITH THOMAS

Keith Thomas was born in 1947. In 1964 he was apprenticed to Ken Preater at Holland & Holland. After completing his apprenticeship in 1969, he stayed at Holland's another eight years. In 1977 he went freelance and moved to the Aylesbury area. Initially he worked for Holland & Holland, but now he works for much of the London trade. Although skilled in all branches of engraving, he has a particular interest in eighteenth-century styles and specialist skills, such as the inletting of silver wire into woodwork.

Keith Thomas at work on a Purdey pair . . .

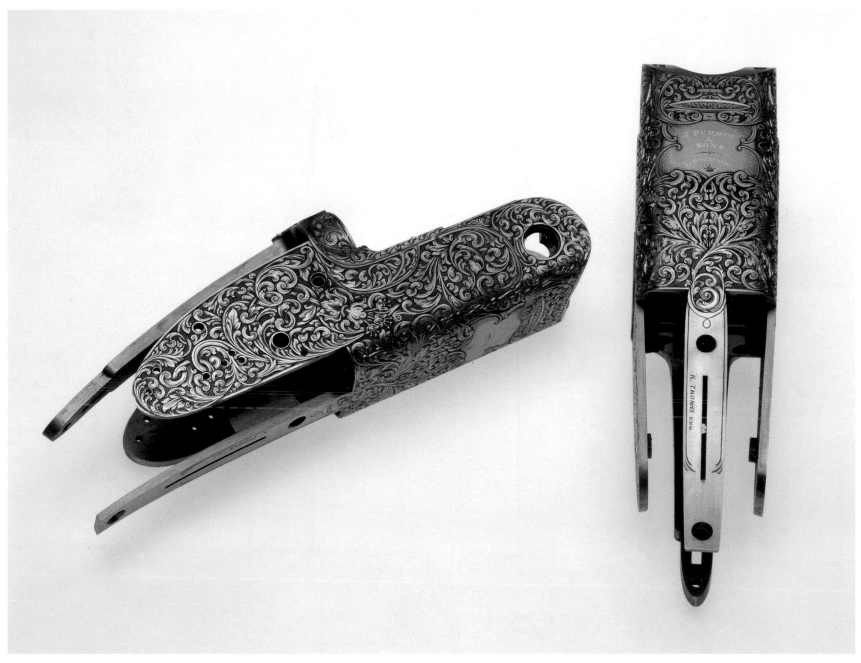

. . . and the Purdey pair he is working on.

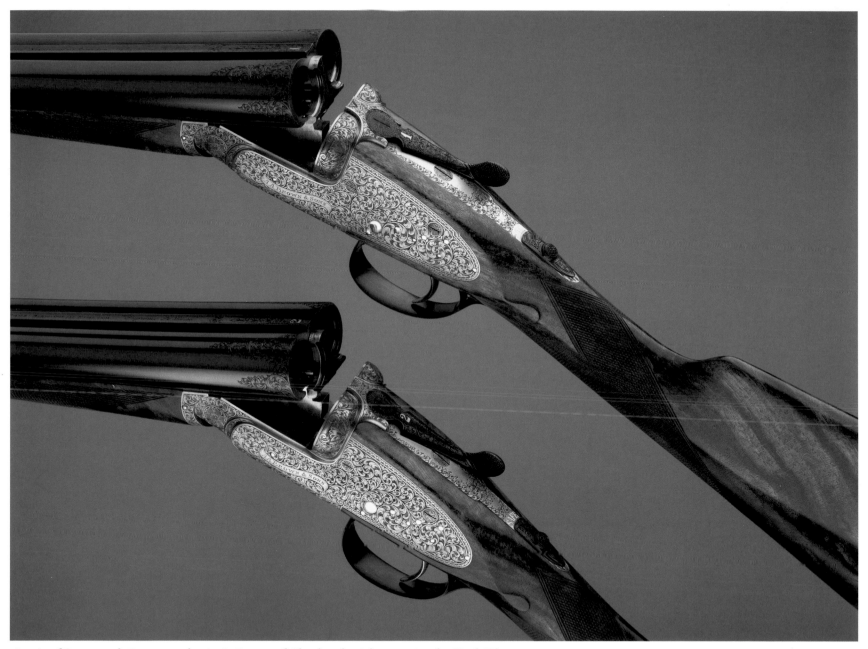

A pair of Supreme de Luxe guns by A. A. Brown of Alvechurch with engraving by Keith Thomas.

Opposite page: A Boss-style over-and-under by Peter V. Nelson with a modern take on Jack Sumner-style engraving by Keith Thomas.

A pair of Peter V. Nelson round-bodied guns with beavertail forearms and fine bouquet and scroll engraving by Keith Thomas.

BRIAN WISEMAN

Brian Wiseman may have learnt engraving from Harry Morris. He now works in Cannock, Staffordshire. NFIA.

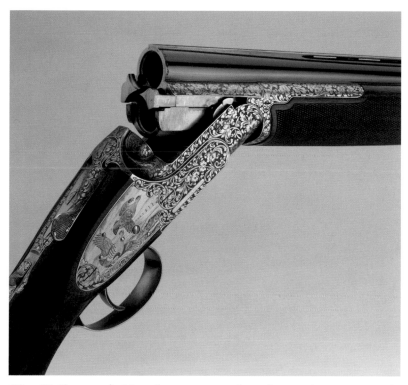

The underside of the Holloway & Naughton gun with engraving by Brian Wiseman.

The Holloway & Naughton over-and-under with engraving by Brian Wiseman.

The following is a list of known engravers who either failed to respond to our queries or did not provide photographs of their work. I have used the abbreviation NFIA (no further information available) and NPOW (no photographs of work).

PETER FRENETTE

Peter Frenette lives in Huntingdonshire and has worked for Asprey. NFIA.

STEPHEN KELLY

Stephen Kelly lives in Essex and has engraved guns for Purdey. NFIA.

CHARLES LEE

Charles Lee lives in Sussex and has engraved guns for Tony R. White and David McKay Brown. NFIA.

DANNY O'BRIEN

Danny O'Brien was born in Paddington in 1944. He attended school at St. Marylebone and apprenticed at Purdey's with Ken Hunt. He worked for Purdey for twenty years before going freelance; he has engraved for Holland & Holland, Boss & Co., John Wilkes, and Westley Richards. NFIA.

KEN PREATER

Ken Preater apprenticed with Bob Corbett at Holland & Holland starting in 1953. After performing his national service in the RAF he returned to H&H in 1960 and eventually became head of their engraving department. He lives near Ascot. NFIA.

RASHID EL HADI

Rashid El Hadi was born in the Sudan in 1961. He came to the U.K. in 1965 and attended St. George's School, Harpenden. He spent several holidays with his cousin, Malcolm Appleby. It was at Malcolm's home that he first encountered the art of engraving, and after some initial instruction from his cousin, he largely taught himself the art. After a term at Sir John Cass College in London in the early 1980s, he joined John Wilkes in 1983, having proved his skill by copying an engraving from a Kell-engraved boxlock. After two years with John Wilkes, he decided to freelance. Purdey's initially employed him, but commissions from Symes & Wright, Rigby, Holland & Holland, and Peter Chapman soon followed. In 1997 he joined Westley Richards, where he is currently specializing in intricate gold inlay, steel carving, and steel piercing. NPOW.

KERRY L. SMITH

Kerry Smith was born in 1973 in Kettering and grew up in Burton Latimer. At sixteen, she left school and started at the Sir John Cass School, where she studied jewelry and silversmithing one day a week for three years. She joined Holland & Holland in 1993 as an apprentice engraver and started to engrave guns after only six months. After three years with Holland & Holland, she left and found work at Watson brothers. Since 1997, she has been working freelance. NPOW.

K. J. SPIBEY

K. J. Spibey who lives in Northwich, Cheshire, has engraved guns for J. Roberts & Son. NFIA.